Previous title by a

Schneider, S. D. (2010)
Mexican Community Health and the Politics of Health Reform,
Albuquerque, University of New Mexico Press.
ISBN 978-0826348869

Meeting the Moment with Kindness

How mindfulness can help us find calm, stability, and an open heart

Meeting the Moment with Kindness

How mindfulness can help us find calm,
stability, and an open heart

By Sue Schneider, Ph.D.

MANTRA
BOOKS

Winchester, UK
Washington, USA

JOHN HUNT PUBLISHING

First published by Mantra Books, 2023
Mantra Books is an imprint of John Hunt Publishing Ltd., No. 3 East Street, Alresford
Hampshire SO24 9EE, UK
office@jhpbooks.com
www.johnhuntpublishing.com
www.mantra-books.net

For distributor details and how to order please visit the 'Ordering' section on our website.

Text copyright: Sue Schneider 2022

ISBN: 978 1 80341 328 0
978 1 80341 329 7 (ebook)
Library of Congress Control Number: 2022913814

A CIP catalogue record for this book is available from the British Library.

Design: Lapiz Digital Services

UK: Printed and bound by CPI Group (UK) Ltd, Croydon, CR0 4YY
Printed in North America by CPI GPS partners

We operate a distinctive and ethical publishing philosophy in
all areas of our business, from our global network of authors to
production and worldwide distribution.

To Aidan, may you always remember to stay present, curious and openhearted.

We shall not cease from exploration
And the end of all our exploring
Will be to arrive where we started
And know the place for the first time
—T.S. Eliot

Contents

Acknowledgements

Writing *Meeting the Moment with Kindness* has been an act of love, fed by the generosity, wisdom and support of others. This book would not have come to fruition without the love and encouragement of my husband and life partner, Brendon. He patiently supported my long hours of writing, offered invaluable input on countless drafts and generously made retreat arrangements when he saw that I needed a break. His love and support helped to light my way.

So many teachers have inspired and encouraged me along my path. I am especially grateful to Tara Brach and Jack Kornfield who ignited my journey 20 years ago. Their two-year training program of which I was recently a part has been such a gift both personally and professionally and has motivated me to carry the mantle of Insight Meditation forward. I also want to acknowledge and appreciate my MBSR teachers, Jeff Brantley and Jeanne van Gemert, formerly at Duke Integrative Medicine, and the Triangle Insight Meditation Community in Durham, for their dedication to supporting meditators at all stages of their practice.

I offer great appreciation and gratitude to Drala (formerly Shambhala) Mountain Center in Red Feather Lakes, CO, which became my space of refuge during the years of writing. There I had the opportunity to train with wise and devoted teachers including David Chernikoff, Susan Kaiser Greenland and Nashalla Nyinda who influenced me in different spheres of my life and practice. The energy of the land in which this center sits has perhaps been the most inspiring teacher of all. Observing its rebirth after the devastating impacts of the Cameron Peak Fire in 2020 taught me firsthand about the transformative power of hope and resilience. I hope you, the reader, will feel its energy and magic spilling into the pages that follow.

I am grateful to all of my students who have brought their presence and curiosity to my classes, raising powerful questions that have led me to profound new levels of insight. I am privileged to be able to continuously learn from such a wise and dedicated community. I also offer gratitude to my coaching clients—past and current—who revealed to me so many different ways that we encounter, resist and befriend the obstacles in our way. I admire their courage and vulnerability and hope that this book can be a resource for them and others on the path.

A special thanks to my book coach, Kelly Madrone, who offered her wisdom and gentle feedback every step of the way. It was through Kelly's encouragement that my own stories found their voice in these pages. I also offer appreciation to Devon Hase, my mentor for two years in the Mindfulness Meditation Teacher Certification Program, who not only inspired me through her dedication to the path, but who offered critical input, insights and encouragement on an earlier draft of this book. A heartfelt thanks goes to two special people in my life, Suzanne Kent, who offered me enduring friendship and faith in my "extracurricular activity," and Laurel Lagoni, who empowered me to believe in myself and inspired me to dream big.

Finally, I offer deep gratitude to my son, Aidan, for motivating me to see this project to fruition. Aidan contributed in so many ways to this book: by cheering me on, cheering me up and sharing his wisdom in our daily conversations. My greatest hope is that his generation and those to follow will embrace the teachings of mindfulness and choose to lead with kindness so that our world may find its way back to balance.

Introduction

The world cannot ruffle the dignity of a soul that dwells in its own tranquility.
—John O'Donohue

We all face major turning points in our lives when we need tools and supports to help us navigate rough waters. Becoming a mom 13 years ago was one of those junctures for me. I found myself overwhelmed and disoriented as I attempted to manage an entirely new set of priorities and responsibilities. As is often the case for new moms, I dropped all self-care, including my longstanding daily meditation practice, and turned my full attention to the endless juggle of caregiving and full-time work. I didn't realize it then, but I had stepped out of the river of mindfulness to focus on the new urgencies in my life.

There was a point in that first year when I recognized that I was not doing well. I wasn't drawing on the tools that could help me center, ground and calm my nervous system. My mind was constantly churning, and I couldn't turn off the "doing" button. So, I enrolled in a mindfulness-based stress reduction program and surrendered myself to the teachings and practices that held me like a life raft. I returned my awareness to my breathing, sent compassion to my tired arms and anxious mind during body scans and felt my feet "kiss" the earth in walking meditation. With a renewed commitment to practice, I started coming home again, to myself, even if only for brief moments. It was enough to help me relocate my internal compass and to step back into the river of mindfulness, even as my world was radically changing.

There are no shortages of stressors in our lives. We wouldn't be human if we could live an existence of perfect ease and tranquility. But what mindfulness teaches us, and what we

1

can experience when we practice in earnest, is that we have a strong, steady, reliable core that we can return to regardless of the waves in our lives. And in the midst of chaos, there can be calm.

One of my favorite mindfulness teaching stories captures this truth eloquently. It goes something like this:

The King of the land announced that he would be holding a contest to see who could make the most beautiful, peaceful painting representing tranquility. Many of the great artists who lived in the village submitted paintings to the King. They were beautiful, calm, pastoral scenes. Yet, none of them met the King's satisfaction.

The people heard rumors that there was a poor peasant who lived far away and that he had some talent. So, they went to him and told him that he should make a painting for the King. The peasant agreed. As it was unveiled, the villagers gasped. What? This is not a tranquil painting! They saw a roaring waterfall. It was crashing and foaming with fury and strength. It was not a waterfall that they would choose to stand under. So, they looked at the peasant with confusion.

"You have to get really close," the peasant told them. They all looked really close at the painting. Sure enough, there was a little gap where the water came down and went around a rock. And in that gap, there was a little ledge with a bird sitting on its eggs in its nest very peacefully. The peasant won the contest.[1]

It is stunning to realize how rarely we notice the tranquil bird sitting on the ledge amidst the crashing, foaming waterfall of life. We more often notice the roaring waterfall. But the tranquil bird is always there. It needs nothing more than our attention, our awareness, to make itself known. And *how* we pay attention matters.

This book is about how to pay attention, on purpose, to our everyday moments, and what can happen—in our brains, bodies, nervous systems, relationships, life trajectories—if we practice this art and take it to heart. On the surface, mindfulness is so simple that it is almost laughable that we have to enroll in workshops, programs and retreats to learn how to quiet our minds and bodies. And yet our capacity to pay attention to our internal and external landscapes is perhaps the most complex, profound and impactful skill we can develop in our lifetime.

What Is Mindfulness?

Mindfulness is an ancient art—a practice, a set of attitudes, a way of being—that has long been available to help humanity wake up to our true nature—our goodness, compassion, caring and relatedness. In Pali, the ancient language of the Buddha, the word for mindfulness is Sati which can be translated as both "awareness" and "remembering." It is the awareness that helps us see more clearly what is within and around us. It is also the wakefulness that reminds us of who we are.

As mindfulness moves through the West, touching people in all walks of life, it is at once critically vital and profoundly misunderstood. It is misunderstood to be limited to the formal practice of meditation, the imagined yogi sitting cross-legged on a cushion with an empty mind and peaceful heart. There are many ways to practice mindfulness and rather than leading to peace and bliss, it more often makes us aware of our restless mind and unsettled heart. This awareness, when met with kindness, is our starting point and our path to greater freedom of heart and mind.

Mindfulness is critically important because, both on the cushion and in daily life, it helps us see the contents of our minds and hearts, which typically remain veiled from our everyday awareness. When we are open and receptive to our inner landscape, we can recognize the unconscious mental patterns that maintain our habitual behaviors and block us from true insight and connection. Mindful awareness can shine light on the fear, attachments and aversions that keeps us caught in cycles of suffering. It can also reveal our inherent stability and the gold that resides just below our awareness. As Tibetan Buddhist teacher Chögyam Trungpa Rinpoche notes, the point of our practice is to "rediscover our hidden neurosis and our hidden sanity at the same time" (2018, p. 53).

Many of us don't know much about our inner landscape—the thoughts we habitually repeat, the stories and narratives we come to believe, the unfelt grief or loss that has been exiled within us or the unacknowledged longing in our hearts. We get intoxicated by busyness, attached to our defenses and locked into stances of denial, shame and blame. We turn away from our emotions and close off from our hearts, denying ourselves and others the caring, love and compassion that is needed. Mindfulness can help us recognize our patterns, shift our perspective and remember who we really are—wise, caring and loving beings. There are profound implications for living closer to our hearts. Mindfulness can be powerful medicine for our times.

I don't write these words lightly or without deep personal experience. Throughout this book, I share how my adult life has been shaped by what I have experienced and learned through my mindfulness journey. My journey consists of almost two decades of exploration and practice in the Insight Meditation tradition and a decade of teaching mindfulness in university and community settings. My practice has been sustained and strengthened through the gifts and challenges of living my ordinary life, particularly as a 50-year-old Caucasian middle-class woman, a wife in a 20-year plus marriage, a mother of a middle-school child and a working parent. Within these roles, I have encountered each of the challenges and obstacles to mindfulness that I describe in this book. I have come to view my day-to-day life as an endless opportunity for practice and exploration.

Insight Meditation, or Vipassana, originated from the Theravada tradition of Southeast Asia, the oldest existing school of Buddhism, which has its roots in India. It offers practitioners a systematic way to cultivate clear awareness or insight into the "true nature of reality," to see things as they are, free of distortion. This method of meditation helps us practice self-observation by anchoring our attention on the breath or physical sensations of the body and observing thoughts and emotions as they come and go, without judgment. In a commonly cited definition offered by Jon Kabat-Zinn, mindfulness is the "awareness that arises through paying attention, on purpose, in the present moment, non-judgmentally."

Not surprisingly, this is a challenging undertaking for many of us, given how we are hardwired and culturally influenced to *not* pay attention. Once we begin to explore our thoughts, feelings and sensations, we often bump up against a number of barriers that seem to impede our practice of mindfulness. This book unpacks some of the common obstacles that we encounter as we embark upon our mindfulness journey. It offers the perspective, as many wisdom traditions do, that our perceived obstacles can become our greatest opportunities for deepening our awareness, insight and access to wisdom and compassion. As is commonly pointed out in mindfulness circles: What is in the way, is the way.

I draw on neuroscience, psychology, contemplative studies and compassion research to ground this exploration in the evolving science of mindfulness. I share my personal experiences, classic Buddhist teachings, insights from my meditation students and the wisdom that my son, Aidan, consistently imparts to me in service of my own process of unearthing and removing obstacles to clear seeing. At the end of each chapter, I offer brief practices that can help to bring awareness to our habituated patterns and our breath, thoughts and body as we connect with our heart and the emotions we store. I emphasize that when we imbue our practice with presence and curiosity, we can develop the inner resources we need to navigate our obstacles from a place of strength, stability and deeper knowing.

I began writing this book as a companion for an online program called Living Mindfully that I developed in 2017 for Colorado State University. I wanted to offer my students a pragmatic, secular and systematic way for learning about mindfulness and applying it in our busy, chaotic lives. Midway through writing the book, the COVID-19 pandemic hit along with a heightened global state of crisis that has only continued to intensify. I turned to my mindfulness practice more than ever before as a means to open up space for the pain and grief that I had difficulty processing. As my awareness was heightened to the suffering of the collective, I began offering my mindfulness classes with a deeper sense of urgency. I completed this book with the same sense of urgency but also a profound well of hope, knowing that humanity has always found its way back from crisis through its inherent wisdom and innate compassion.

I never suggest to my students that mindfulness can ameliorate any of their problems or the problems facing our world. Instead, I suggest that the power of its medicine lies in helping us relate to these problems with greater perspective and equanimity. I emphasize the importance of developing mindfulness as a critical foundation for wise action. To this end, I find Tibetan Buddhist teacher Yongey Mingyur Rinpoche's words particularly instructive:

"People everywhere try too hard to make the world better. Their intentions are admirable, yet they seek to change everything but themselves. To make yourself a better person is to make the world a better place... Until we transform ourselves, we are like mobs of angry people screaming for peace. In order to move the world, we must be able to stand still in it" (2019, p. 104).

Standing still in the present moment is not easy but, as we will see, it is an abundantly fruitful place of self-discovery and the birthplace of wise action.

An Unexpected Discovery

Mindfulness meditation found me when I was least expecting it. I was living in a small town in Mexico, facing down my dissertation research as a budding anthropologist. My project entailed observing groups of *promotoras* who were employing an array of healing practices in community clinics throughout Central Mexico. They were offering acupuncture, Reiki and massage along with Mexican herbal medicine and *limpias* or energy clearings which were traditional practices that they claimed they were "rescuing" from a rapidly urbanizing Mexican culture (Schneider, 2010).

Given the global array of modalities they were practicing, it wasn't surprising when one of the *promotoras*, Angelica, announced a week-long meditation retreat to be held in their community center. Angelica had met an American woman in Mexico City who was teaching meditation that summer in Mexico. After hearing about the healing work that these groups were offering in the community, this teacher agreed to offer a retreat in their town of Yautepec.

When Angelica first asked me to join the retreat, my immediate reaction was, "I don't have time to spend a week meditating!" But she was persistent, knowing that I would benefit from the experience. While I was resistant, I was equally curious about how this ancient Eastern practice would be taught, translated and interpreted by this group of Catholic Mexican health promoters. So, I accepted the invitation and it turned out to be one of the best decisions I have ever made.

The week wasn't easy by any means. I spent it struggling. I struggled to concentrate. I struggled to focus on my breath. I struggled to allow what I was feeling to happen. But as the days wore on, I also tapped into some things I hadn't felt before. Moments of relief from anxiety. A deep stillness. A glimpse that my all-important research and my desires and needs weren't as important as I thought they were. Later in the week as I listened to this group of women burst out in joyous singing in the middle of one of our practice sessions, I sensed that something radically important was happening. These women had a way to collectively express their experience of opening to life. I glowed for weeks after that experience, in awe of the joy that erupted through our shared experience and amazed at how free I could feel when I was fully present.

I stuck with the daily meditation practices that I learned that week. When I returned to Michigan to write up my dissertation, my curiosity about meditation was in full bloom. I found a weekly meditation group and jumped in with both feet. Through books that our group read together, I was introduced to meditation teachers like Jack Kornfield, Tara Brach, Sharon Salzberg and Pema Chödrön, all who would have a significant impact in my life and some with whom I'd formally study.

In those early years, I had great hope that my practice would help me better manage my stress, anxiety and exhausting perfectionist tendencies. I expected that meditation would help me shore up my insecurities and "fix" my relationship struggles. It did and it didn't. No difficulties in my life have ever been "resolved" through mindfulness. I still get overwhelmed, stressed out, blocked and stuck in relationship ruts. But now, rather than despising the difficult, messy aspects of my life, I see them as fodder for helping me become more self-aware. I have learned to relate more kindly to myself and to whatever life puts in front of me. When the inevitable challenges, fears, insecurities and doubts arise, I know what to do. I can slow things down and observe my thoughts and emotions with kind attention. I can drop the story and release my desire for things to be a certain way. The gifts of my practice continue to manifest in ways I could never have imagined, and I share some of what I have learned in this book.

Sitting Still in a Busy World

Since that auspicious week in Mexico in 2003, I have made mindfulness a central component of my life both personally and professionally. While I meditate daily, this is just a small aspect of my mindfulness practice. I try regularly to bring mindful awareness into my relationships, work and parenting along with all of my daily decisions and actions. Formally on the cushion and informally during my daily routine, I remind myself again and again to slow down, notice my breath and bring awareness to my thoughts, feelings and body. I've been on this journey for many years. It's still challenging, and I spend plenty of time acting mindlessly. But I have learned firsthand that intention goes a long way.

My son, Aidan, has grown up knowing that his parents' bedtime routine always involves meditation. He is used to seeing my husband, Brendon, and I, sitting on our cushions, eyes closed, at the end of the day whether we are at home or on vacation. Brendon is also a mindfulness instructor (and a therapist), so mindfulness is often in the foreground or background of our conversations, meals, walks and interactions with others — from the perspective of how we succeed or neglect to bring our most mindful selves to the moment. Given the prominence of mindfulness in our family, it's been interesting to occasionally check in with Aidan to see what he thinks about our practice and mindfulness in general. When I asked him a few years ago why he thought Mom and Dad meditated, his answer was this:

I think you guys meditate to reach that peace in your body. After everything you guys do every day, I think it feels like you need to get it out and have twenty minutes of peace in the world.

What a good start for a then 11-year-old! When I asked my meditation students why they meditate, some of their responses included:

- It makes me feel like me
- To settle more deeply into myself
- To become something better
- To get over the hump of difficulties
- To learn how to take care of myself

While people's expectations of and experiences with meditation can be diverse, it is fair to say that this list contains some of the things we long for in our busy, frenetic lives which are often spent distracted and distanced from our authentic selves. Only when we get still and silent and we open up space to the many thoughts, feelings and sensations that arise in any given moment, can we find some sense of balance and heart-connection with ourselves.

As Aidan suggests, our practice can help us reach peace in our body and find moments of calm in the world. But mindfulness offers us no guarantees. It is just as likely that when we sit in stillness, rather than touching peace, we tap directly into our judging, busy, restless mind. When I recently described to my students the Five Classic Hinderances that we regularly encounter when we sit down to meditate—grasping, aversion, restlessness, sleepiness and doubt—they collectively sighed a breath of relief as if to say, "You mean, I'm not the only one caught in these mind storms when I'm assuming everyone around me is basking in peace?" A handful privately wrote notes of gratitude in the chat box for relieving them of their unrealistic expectations.

Despite the challenges of sitting still in a busy world with agitated and restless minds, we still practice. Why? Perhaps because those of us who have sat on our cushion for any period of time intuitively know that there is no way around life's difficulties and messiness, that we must go through it. And the only way through it is by learning about and leaning into our own internal messiness. As we observe our internal landscape, we begin to see our patterns, habits and hang-ups. Our means of self-protection, internal dialogues, stories, narcissism and attachments are all revealed in full view.

At the same time, as we cultivate compassion in our practice, we learn how to be gentle with ourselves and care for and nurture those imperfect, wounded and rejected parts. As we learn to quiet the voices, calm the storms and settle the nervous system, our hearts can begin to experience what it's like to come home to our true selves, our essential nature, the ultimate gift of presence. It takes persistence and a willingness to open to what is real. We may only catch glimpses of what lies beyond the small self, but those glimpses can be powerful markers, keeping us on the path.

A Global and Timely Offering

With its 2,500-year-old roots in the East, mindfulness has "taken off" in the West over the last few decades. Buddhism has long been part of the diversity of American culture as Asian immigrants brought teachings and practices from their traditions to the U.S. as early as the 1800s. A shift occurred in the 1970s with the steady influx of meditation teachers from the East traveling to the West to share their teachings. At the same time, many Westerners began traveling to Asian countries for formal training in meditation and bringing the teachings home.

The seeds of secular mindfulness were planted in the U.S. by Jon Kabat-Zinn who launched the mindfulness-based stress reduction (MBSR) program in 1979. Kabat-Zinn's clinical research broke ground in establishing the scientific validity of mindfulness as an approach for addressing clinical and nonclinical issues. Now there are secular meditation groups, classes, teachers and centers in almost every U.S. city. Many medical centers, universities, public schools and businesses pay for their employees to attend mindfulness programs. My work reflects the growing acceptability of mindfulness in American culture as I teach mindfulness classes within the university and throughout the community in my role as an Extension educator at Colorado State University (CSU). I am joined by many like-minded colleagues involved with the CSU Center for Mindfulness who are insistent that mindfulness is an essential and critical skill for all individuals to develop at any life stage.

Mindfulness has long been a global phenomenon, as I first witnessed in my introduction to meditation in Mexico. Now, students from all over the world, including Buddhist countries, are coming to the U.S. to learn mindfulness meditation. For example, in 2019, I joined hundreds of international and U.S. students who came together in Washington, D.C., for the opening weekend of a two-year Mindfulness Meditation Teaching Certification Program (MMTCP) taught by Jack Kornfield and Tara Brach. The students in my cohort have since graduated and are teaching mindfulness all over the world.

COVID-19 began its spread during my two-year program and our global cohort found ourselves connected in more ways than just our shared passion for teaching mindfulness. We were fortunate to have been offered powerful teachings and instruction for helping our students (and ourselves) manage the fear, loss and uncertainty that marked those turbulent times. Like other teachers, I quickly moved my weekly face-to-face meditation classes to Zoom. Mindfulness teachers across the world were adapting their approach to meet the complex and virtual realities of our new world. As a result, there has been an explosion of mindfulness offerings that are now accessible to individuals everywhere who have access to the internet. According to *Forbes* Magazine, mindfulness "came of age" in 2020 as a result of COVID-19. This has been a particularly prolific time for the spread of secular mindfulness and its adaptation to meet the urgency of the present moment.

Times Are Urgent

The pandemic and all that followed both challenged my capacity for mindfulness and pushed it ruthlessly to new depths. Like many others, I experienced many powerful emotions that came out of the discomfort of not knowing what lay ahead and an uncomfortable sense of groundlessness. The waves of 2020 just kept crashing, with videos of racial violence and protests, images of devastating fires, the swelling COVID-19 death toll, political upheaval, senseless massacres and the list goes on.

Early in the pandemic, I discovered a phrase from Nigerian activist Bayo Akomolafe that instructed me through the waves of crises: "The times are urgent; let us slow down." I repeated the phrase everywhere I went: The times are urgent; let us slow down. In my meditation classes: The times are urgent; let us slow down. At the grocery store: The times are urgent; let us slow down. During my frenetic workdays: The times are urgent; let us slow down.

I spent time feeling the contrast of these two phrases in my body; I noticed the impulse of my body propelling me toward action while the wisdom of my body was imploring me to slow down. As Akomolafe points out, slowing down seems like the absolute wrong thing to do when there's a fire on the mountain.[2] But, as our mindfulness practice shows us, the fire on the mountain *is* part of life. We can't wish it away or extinguish it by will. It burns through at its own pace. When we slow down, we become aware enough to tune into the fire, to notice its trajectory and the sensation of its heat and to recognize what action to take in the moment. By slowing down, we can see what is actually happening within and around us rather than reacting from fear. This is one example of clear seeing.

It's not just pandemics, fires and senseless death that highlights the rationale for slowing down during urgent times. Too often, we let our precious lives pass by unnoticed. Both during times of crisis and times of calm, our lives are desperately awaiting our attention. Our breath is waiting to be noticed. Our hearts are waiting to be felt. If we don't pay attention, we continue to wander through our lives half asleep. These are urgent matters. Our lives are precious. Mindfulness helps us slow down.

Pragmatic Mindfulness

Slowing down is the first step in seeing ourselves and our lives clearly. It is also one of the biggest challenges we face as we begin to cultivate mindfulness. Our ability to pause and notice what is happening within and around us is critical for developing what I describe in this book as pragmatic mindfulness. This refers to mindfulness that we develop and apply in our everyday, ordinary lives to help us discover who we are, how we can relate consciously to whatever is happening and how we bring about wise, mindful action. Most of us cannot spend weeks or months in silent meditation retreats. But we can dedicate ourselves to a regular meditation practice and apply the principles of mindfulness every day in our homes, workplaces and communities.

Pragmatic mindfulness is not a self-improvement project; we are not trying to fix anything that is wrong with ourselves, our lives or the world. We are simply slowing down and becoming aware, knowing that clear seeing proceeds wise actions. There are many traditions and practices that can help us cultivate mindful awareness, many paths up the mountain, as they say. I describe a particular path through teachings and practices that I have found extraordinarily helpful in my life.

Taking up the "practice" of directly observing our experience is critically important for developing mindful awareness. We are told that the Buddha instructed his students to not believe what he said about the benefits of mindfulness but to see for themselves through their practice. Here, practicing doesn't mean doing something again and again so we can get better at it, like playing tennis or the piano. Certainly, the more we practice meditation, the stronger our "mindfulness muscle" gets. But we are not trying to get anywhere. Mindfulness is fundamentally a non-striving agenda. We practice to become aware of our attachments and aversions, our stories and judgments, to be able to see things as they really are. If there is a "goal" of our practice, it is to notice all of the ways that we get in our own way of seeing clearly who we are and what is happening in the moment, in our lives and in the world.

This book explores the many ways we get stalled and stuck as we develop mindful awareness and the steps we can take toward freeing ourselves. It offers many examples of how we meet our obstacles on the mindfulness path as opportunities for developing a richer, deeper connection with ourselves and the world around us. This connection can be a gateway to discovering our true nature—our gold. Our mindfulness journey, however, does not stop with self-discovery. Bringing mindful awareness into our everyday lives helps us widen our lens, see the world more clearly and know how to be in wise relationship with our hurting world.

Each chapter explores a specific aspect of mindfulness that we can cultivate by: Bringing awareness to unconscious, habitual patterns (Chapter 1), pausing and attuning to our internal landscape (Chapter 2), responding rather than reacting to our stressors (Chapter 3), transforming negative and judgmental habits (Chapter 4), turning toward our feelings and emotions (Chapter 5), surrendering to groundlessness (Chapter 6) and opening our hearts to ourselves and the world (Chapter 7). When these aspects of mindfulness are left unattended in our lives, our capacity for clear seeing can be diminished. When we bring curiosity and friendliness to what appears to be in our way, profound opportunities for wisdom and growth emerge.

Chapter 1

Meeting Our Unconscious Habits

Beauty is the harvest of presence.
—David Whyte

When Aidan was a toddler, he loved stomping through puddles and making big splashes. He would grin from ear to ear looking down at his bright yellow rain boots submerged in water. As children, we have great capacity for being present in the moment. We notice the grass between our toes and when a bug is on the move. We are happy dancing in the rain and diving headfirst into the snow. But we tend to lose that ability as we get older. We get busy with school and careers, with partners and parenting. We become consumed with our identities, problems and properties. We focus on the future and the things we need to do. Put simply, we get busy *doing*. And we forget about *being*.

When I returned to Michigan after spending a year in Mexico, I was still fresh from the week-long meditation retreat and my new mindfulness practice. I appreciated being able to catch glimpses of what it was like to *be* again. Sitting in silence, noticing my breath and walking mindfully helped me touch into moments of simply *being* in my body. The moments were fleeting but they were enough to help me maintain my commitment to my budding practice. I sought out a meditation group that met weekly at the local hospital and began practicing with a small, dedicated group of practitioners. We would do sitting meditation together followed by reading passages from books of Buddhist wisdom and we'd close with a short sitting practice.

I didn't find the sitting easy. During our meditations, I would notice a consistent pattern of anxiety and dizziness that would arise as I would try to settle in. My mind would spin out of control, and I would get lost in anxious thoughts. I never knew what kind of discomfort I would face from one week to the next. There were times in which I felt like my brain would explode; no matter what I did, I couldn't steady my mind or quiet my thoughts. I would hear the voice of a wise teacher in my head saying, "Don't try so hard!" I would try to relax but soon find myself tensing up again. But I stayed with the practice, following the instructions for anchoring in my breath and noticing what was happening with as little judgment as possible.

The struggles I faced in my nascent meditation practice were mirrored in my struggles to apply the principles of mindfulness in my everyday life. I was tense and anxious, in the throes of writing my dissertation, feeling underqualified to teach my classes and worried about if I could eventually land a "real" job. My internal demons were raging, bringing out the worst of my inner critic, insecurities and perfectionist tendencies. They were all bundled together in a voice that said, "Get it done perfectly but don't fool yourself that you'll succeed."

These voices propelled me to maintain unhealthy work habits and they perpetuated my anxiety. I didn't have enough awareness at the time to know that I was operating out of deep conditioning and internalized messages I had been strengthening since my childhood. Nor did I understand that the more I pushed away my anxiety about failure, the stronger it became. I was learning about meditation intellectually and diligently practicing but somehow was not able to apply mindfulness in my life.

It is easy to let our unexamined conditioning and unconscious habits direct our actions. We develop our habits in childhood and strengthen them as we age. Without awareness, these habits can manifest in sneaky and underhanded ways throughout our lives. My perfectionism and anxiety had been with me for many years, but they went into overdrive when I was in graduate school. These energies fought a fierce and valiant battle against my efforts to relax and to cultivate presence during my early efforts at meditation. It was only through years of practice that I was able to develop enough awareness that I could see these patterns clearly, begin to unwind them and open up space for a different way of being.

Mindfulness can help us bring our habituated patterns and behaviors out of the shadows. These habits can serve as huge obstacles to living more mindfully. But they can also become great teachers and offer opportunities for growth. When we see our habits with greater awareness, we recognize that they are made up of thoughts that aren't necessarily true or useful and beliefs we've developed to protect ourselves and feel safe.

Our mindfulness practice can help us to become familiar with our habits and patterns so that we don't have to blindly follow them. Learning to cultivate "presence," or the ability to be awake and aware in the moment, is what helps us to see our habits with greater clarity. As our presence deepens, so too does our capacity for clear seeing. And as we see more clearly that our habits are just mental imprints that are not static or solid, we can learn how to release their grip. When we aren't blindly reacting to our unconscious habits of *doing*, we are more able to *be*. We can't grow younger or revert back to our simpler childhood ways. But we can re-learn what it means to be present and available in our lives. We can learn to develop mindfulness.

Assumptions About Mindfulness

In my years of teaching mindfulness, I have heard many misinterpretations about what it is. So, I like to share a classic cartoon when I introduce the topic. The cartoon shows a person with a thought bubble filled with lots of symbols representing thoughts. The dog standing next to him has a perfectly empty thought bubble. Just grass and a blue sky. The juxtaposition is relatable, but it offers a false dichotomy. I've always told my students that if their minds are truly empty, they are probably dogs. Attaining a quiet, blue-sky mind is not the point of mindfulness, nor is it possible for most of us. Instead, mindfulness encompasses the process of *learning* to become aware of our busy mind and all of its contents. This process is not about rejecting or getting rid of thoughts but rather cultivating an accepting awareness.

I like to draw a pair of eyeglasses gazing down at the busy mind in the cartoon. Adding an observer's lens to the picture helps us see what we are doing when we practice mindfulness: we are becoming a witness to our internal landscape. How does this happen? We first need to anchor our attention and a good place to anchor is our breath, although there are other anchors like the hands, feet or sounds. When we are anchored and present, we can notice the rising and falling away of thoughts, emotions and sensations. We can become aware of mental chatter, physical sensations and emotional energy that usually lie beneath our awareness. As an observer or witness to our minds and bodies, so much more becomes available to our conscious mind than was available before. We notice that whatever arises will pass and that things are constantly changing if we pay attention.

The cartoon is helpful in that it highlights many assumptions about mindfulness that need to be undone. For example, the two thought bubbles that stand in contrast suggest that "busy mind" is bad and "empty mind" is good. But mindfulness, and the Buddhist philosophy that underlies it, does not judge "empty mind" as good or "busy mind" as bad. Instead, if we have busy mind, then we get to know it. Not with the intention of changing it. Simply to get to know it. We might view busy mind (and anxious mind, and sleepy mind, and angry mind) as an opportunity for deepening our awareness, examining our tendency to grasp at pleasing thoughts or reject uncomfortable feelings. We can view whatever comes up—whether they are stressful thoughts, distractions or uncomfortable sensations—as the perfect fodder for our practice, rather than a barrier to peace.

The most common assumption I hear students share is that our mindfulness meditation practice will help us achieve a peaceful Zen state of mind like that of the dog. While we may begin a practice with that hope, our instruction is to let go of striving to achieve any particular state. Why? Because striving does not bring about a desired state; it only brings about attachment to a state. Moreover, we have developed a neocortex that readies our brain for busy, analytic activity. It takes intention and commitment to stay present even for one moment. We can't clear our minds on demand. That takes training in undoing our lifelong habits of following after our thoughts, repeating our stories and fixating on our narratives.

The other reason we let go of our desire for "Zen-dog-mind" in our practice is that our goal is not to squelch or escape our mental chaos. Instead, we are learning how to get curious about it, how to get to know it better. We practice investigating it, without getting swept away by it. Our gentle curiosity about "busy mind" is open rather than judgmental. The magic of mindfulness happens when we remember to return to our stable foundation—our breath or the body in this moment—when we notice that we have strayed away from the present. Like a dog in training, we are learning to stay.

Jon Kabat-Zinn refers to mindfulness in terms of **"coming to our senses."** When we learn how to tune into our bodies, our practice can help us become aware of the most basic sensory experience. We can make contact with sounds, smells, feelings and thoughts, all of which must, by definition, come from our awareness of the body. This is why, in Buddhist philosophy, the body is the first of four foundations of mindfulness, followed by feelings, mind and arising phenomena. In other words, there is no getting around the body.

Imagine drinking a cup of tea. You can feel the warmth of the cup in your hands. You can smell the essence of the tea. You can taste the tea in your mouth. You can notice how you feel as you sip the tea and the warmth moves through your body. There are no future thoughts or worries if you are drinking your tea mindfully. You are simply experiencing the moment in its fullness.

Benedictine monk Brother David Steindl-Rast suggests that being present, awake in our bodies and grateful are inherently connected. A quote on his Gratefulness.org website beautifully captures this connection: "Much of the time we live like disembodied minds, not even noticing what's around us, but preoccupied with past and future. But when this mug of tea warms first our hands and then our stomach on a cold day, or the cat purrs contentedly in our lap, we are suddenly present and grateful." This experience of truly being present offers us gifts, like the accessibility of gratitude, that we may have forgotten are available in the busyness of our everyday lives.

Kabat-Zinn's well-cited definition of mindfulness encapsulates what we are doing when we are sipping our tea in this way: "Mindfulness means paying attention in a particular way: on purpose, in the present moment, and non-judgmentally." The definition doesn't mention outcomes like, "Paying attention so I can achieve a clear, spacious, Zen-like, dog mind." Instead, mindfulness refers to the attitudes, intention and attention that we bring to our practice of becoming aware of this very moment. The process of deepening our awareness is important, not any outcomes we might hope to achieve. The mindfulness path is paved with curiosity rather than expectations about uncovering the hidden, unrealized parts of ourselves.

Attitudes and Attributes of Mindfulness

Kabat-Zinn's definition of mindfulness names key components of our practice that are worth exploring more closely here:

Paying Attention

Paying attention means that we are bringing *awareness* to our moment-to-moment experience. This can be noticing the wind rushing through the trees or it can be following our busy "monkey mind" while we are meditating. Monkey mind refers to the constant chatter in our heads and the unsettled and restless nature of our minds. We only become aware of our busy minds when we stop and pay attention. Sometimes, mindful awareness is referred to as "bare attention." This refers to the idea that we can bring our full attention to the moment without layering on any emotional reactions. In other words, we don't evaluate, judge, grasp or reject the experience. We simply have the experience. And we notice having the experience.

On Purpose

We have a choice about whether or not to pay attention to the squirrels in the trees. Most of the time, we let our minds wander into the future or we ruminate on the past or we repeat familiar stories to ourselves. In these cases, we are disconnected from what is actually happening in the moment. But if we bring an *intention* to stay present for that moment, we are making a different choice. We can choose to pay attention on purpose.

In a Particular Way

Mindfulness also refers to the *attitudes* that we bring to paying attention in the moment. For example, we can bring qualities of curiosity, openness and acceptance to an experience we are having, letting things be just as they are. These qualities might serve us well if we want to see the true nature of what is happening with unbiased eyes and without layers of judgment, resistance or grasping. When we do this, we can see that things continually change: our thoughts come and go like clouds in the sky, our emotions shift and morph like a flowing river, noises come and go as do the sensations in our body. With curiosity, we can stay open to whatever is happening with a fresh perspective.

Non-judgmentally

We tend to label our experiences as either good or bad. We want the good things to last and the bad things to go away. This creates barriers to our unbiased, moment-to-moment presence, in the form of grasping or aversion. We invest a lot of our energy in wanting things to be different from the way they are. While we can't necessarily eliminate our judging mind, if we are practicing mindfulness, we can be aware of when judgments arise and how they cloud our eyes from seeing what is actually happening. We can acknowledge those judgments with kindness rather than aversion, preventing ourselves from judging the judgment.

Paying attention in the present moment, nonjudgmentally, is by no means easy. When we actually start paying attention, through mindful awareness, we notice how distracted and agitated our minds can be. We see how our monkey mind gets in the way of our ability to be present. And because we are so used to getting caught up in our mental activity, it is easy to conclude that the practice of getting to know our monkey mind is "too hard." But, as Mingyur Rinpoche suggests, not paying attention to our minds is like owning a car without knowing how to drive. "The less we know about the chattering, muttering voice in our heads that tells us what to do, what to believe, what to buy, which people we should love, and so forth, the more power we grant it to boss us around and convince us that whatever it says is true" (2019, p. 38).

Our bossy minds can pull us onto streets, highways and racetracks that we never intended to spend time on. We can easily be surprised when we start to notice the speed in which things actually happen and the extent to which we are not present. The first time that my students experience a guided meditation practice, there is inevitably a chorus of people chiming in about how busy their minds are or how good it feels to get quiet for a moment. As Pema Chödrön notes, "We all get so caught up in our habitual patterns that we're not there for the world we're immersed in. When they experience a gap, people often say, wow it's such a big world and I was so tunnel visioned that I didn't even realize the sky was there, and there were birds on the telephone wires."[3] Our mindfulness practice allows us to slow down so that we can notice what is unfolding before us and within us that we would have otherwise missed.

The idea of attending to the present moment can seem easy. So try this. Put the book down for 30 seconds and pay attention to your breath. That's all. Just be with the in-breath and out-breath for 30 seconds. Done. What did you notice? Perhaps that you had 12 thoughts in those 30 seconds? Maybe you noticed that it was a lot of work to stay focused on your breath? Maybe you felt a sense of calm come over you. Practicing mindfulness is by no means passive. To the contrary, the practice requires an *active* intention to stay open and available to what is happening. The cultivation of certain attitudes supports this active and alert effort, as Kabat-Zinn describes in his landmark book *Full Catastrophe Living* (1990). Some of these attitudes include:

- *Trust.* We can learn to trust ourselves and that we can handle whatever comes up including difficulty and discomfort.
- *Patience.* We can trust that things unfold in their own time and learn how to not hurry through one moment to get to the next.
- *Acceptance.* We can adopt a willingness to be open to how things actually are rather than trying to make something different happen.
- *Beginner's mind.* We can learn to see the world with unbiased eyes and a curious mind. Expert mind is the opposite of beginner's mind. If we think we know what is going to happen, we have lost the opportunity to experience the full possibility of the moment.

Mindfulness is neither a passive endeavor, nor is it an exercise in detachment. Quite the opposite. As American Buddhist teacher Larry Rosenberg suggests, mindfulness is a form of participation— "you are fully living out your life but you are awake in the midst of it... It can be used on a simple process like the breathing, or on highly charged and unpleasant emotions like fear or loneliness. It can also follow us into the ordinary life situations that make up our day. Eventually, it becomes more a way of living than a technique" (2004, pp. 15–16). Or, as Kabat-Zinn puts it, "Mindfulness is a way of being in relationship to experience" (2019, p. XIV).

Part of the confusion about mindfulness in our culture has to do with the emphasis that is put on meditation, the formal practice of anchoring the mind and bringing awareness to our thoughts, emotions and sensations. Meditation in its many forms—standing, sitting, walking, body scan—applies all of the principles and attitudes of mindfulness discussed here. While meditation is something that we do as our sole activity, maybe in the morning or before bed or during a silent retreat, mindfulness is something that we bring into our everyday moments and lives as we attend to the present. This is why mindfulness is pragmatic. It is a set of attitudes and approaches that we can apply to all of our activities from washing dishes to driving our car. Our practice and our life are not separate when we bring mindful awareness to the moment.

Recognizing Habits of Mind

Our everyday mindfulness practice is challenging because it is an active stance of being awake in our minds and bodies. It asks us to stay present to what is happening rather than sleepwalking through our days or getting pulled around by our unconscious patterns and habituated behaviors. When we are unaware of these patterns and behaviors, they become obstacles to our mindfulness and our ability to see ourselves clearly. It is helpful to name some of these patterns and habits and explore how they might block us from mindfulness when we are not paying attention.

Life in Three Gears

In our busy lives we tend to spend much of our time in three gears:

1. *Accelerator.* Our foot is on the accelerator and we are speeding through life, going from one thing to another. We're seeking the next pleasurable moment, planning for the next vacation or the next purchase and running toward the next phase of life. All of this happens at warp speed.
2. *Automatic pilot.* We can spend a lot of our time on automatic pilot. We move through life oblivious to what we're doing. We drive without paying attention to where we are going, eat without noticing how our food tastes and overlook the quality of our relationships.
3. *Stuck.* Without paying attention to what we are doing or where we are going, we might find ourselves stuck. We may be in a rut, an unfulfilling job or an unhealthy relationship. We often stay stuck for long periods of time because that sometimes feels easier than putting our effort into making a change.

These gears can become our default modes. They begin to feel normal. They don't force us to notice, experience or do anything differently. We may feel underlying discomfort, that something is just not right, but we may not know what to do about it.

These gears can easily get locked into place when we are not present. Our repeated habits create deep grooves in our brains that keep us returning to the same behaviors again and again. Regardless of whether or not the behaviors serve us, we may continue to enact them because doing so is familiar and familiar is comfortable. Enacting these behaviors can protect us from feeling our unwanted feelings, unmasking pain or trauma that is hidden from view and touching into the longing that lies dormant within.

Mind States

Our habituated patterns often arise from specific mind states that go unrecognized until we shine the light of awareness on them.

Controlling Mind. Our control strategies help us to further keep our discomforts at bay. We stay busy so we can feel that we are in control, particularly in the face of uncertainty. Since life is unavoidably uncertain, our controlling instincts help us cover over the anxiety. As Jack Kornfield (1995) points out, "One of the problems in our society is that we have not learned to distinguish uncertainty from anxiety." If we uncouple the two, we could learn how to be with uncertainty rather than adding a layer of anxiety onto our discomfort. But rather than noticing what is happening, looking for the source of our discomfort or taking kind care of ourselves, we often seek out distractions to soothe our anxiety.

Distracted Mind. To avoid unwanted feelings, we often turn to food, alcohol or substances to temporarily soothe our angst. We might use our electronic devices, social media or activities like overwork or gambling to escape ourselves. We turn to whatever soothing behaviors will help us avoid feeling discomfort and dis-ease. We may grow ashamed of our behaviors but not know how to change. This leads to self-judgment. In other words, we take actions that are intended to make us feel better, but they instead create new barriers to addressing our real needs. We may end up disliking ourselves. This dislike might turn to disgust and even lead to self-hatred.

Judging Mind. We are masterful at judging ourselves negatively and harshly. We may enact behaviors that come from a place of self-protection and fear and our judging minds tend to aggravate our anxiety. This causes us to further avoid, placate or soothe our pain, leading us back to the behaviors that cause shame, and the cycle continues. At the root of our suffering is a sense that we are not enough, and we are inherently "bad." Tara Brach calls this the "trance of unworthiness." It is what we learn as children and through our society and how we experience ourselves through a deficiency lens. When we feel that we are not lovable enough, smart enough, successful enough, etc., we may pursue self-improvement projects that are aimed toward "fixing" our outer selves rather than leaning into and caring for the pain within. This self-improvement mentality further exiles us from our core selves. We might spend our lives operating under the false pretense that these fixes will finally lead us to the inner happiness we're seeking.

Future Happiness Mind. We know that seeking external forms of pleasure will not lead to lasting inner happiness. Research shows that lottery winners only temporarily experience greater happiness after they win. They ultimately return to their emotional "set point" once the novelty wears off. Psychologist Sonja Lyubomirsky (2008) found in her research that 10 percent of what determines our happiness has to do with our outer circumstances. Fifty percent of our happiness relates to our genetic inheritance and forty percent relates to our actions and thought. In other words, we have significant capacity for influencing our wellbeing. Yet we often live our lives as if happiness is only available on account of certain *external* conditions being met in the future... when I get the next promotion, house, partner, etc. So, while waiting for our *real* life to begin, we ignore the richness of our present moments and miss opportunities to experience our life as it is. This disconnect further perpetuates our unhappiness.

Mindfulness as a Mirror

Our tendencies to distract, numb, control, judge and seek happiness through external conditions have one significant thing in common: they reflect our desire for things to be different from how they are. Most of us spend a fair amount of time in conflict with ourselves and our circumstances. My battles with life have led me to feel anxious, angry and helpless at times. As I embarked upon my lifelong journey of becoming aware of and letting go of the conflict, I began freeing up energy that I didn't know existed. I also discovered a core of stillness within me, free from anxiety and discontent, that I could tap into, regardless of my external situation. This was a revelation that has had significant implications for me as I've continued to learn about the conditioning that has long influenced my life.

Our unconscious habits can be powerful forces. When we live with our foot on the accelerator pedal or we are driven by our insecurities, we tend to ignore or reject what our lives are offering right now. We can't get those moments back. These habits and tendencies are pervasive obstacles to being present, but they are not cause for blame. They are natural and protective and have an evolutionary basis, as we will explore in Chapter 4. With practice we can learn how to bring our habituated behaviors into the light of awareness. Mindfulness can serve as a mirror for helping us to see what lies behind our mental habits which is a strong core of unshakeable stability. It's never too late to start paying attention. We are all trainable. As we will see in the next chapter, our training starts with the basics, at the beginning, with re-learning how to simply pause and attune.

***

Practice: Learning to Pay Attention

Find a place to sit comfortably. This might be a chair or sofa or meditation cushion. You might close your eyes and direct your attention to your connection with your seat. Then bring your focus downward to your feet as they touch the floor. You might imagine that you have roots that go down from your body deep into the earth. Notice how well supported you are by the floor. Bringing your attention slowly up your spine, gently straighten your back and release your shoulders, seeing if you can find a relaxed but alert position. From here, you might take a few deep, conscious belly breaths filling the lungs on the inhale and then slowly releasing on the exhale.

Let your breath resume its natural rhythm and rest your attention gently on your breath. Your attention might naturally rest on the rising and falling of the chest or the expanding and contracting of the abdomen. Or the most natural resting place for your attention might be in noticing the cool air coming into your nose and the warm air going out. When you find your "anchor," take a few moments to bring your full attention to the breathing. You are not forcing anything to happen but simply observing the breath while breathing.

Now, let your breath recede into the background and invite your awareness to notice the array of sensations in your body. Do you feel tingling or tightness? Are there places in your body that want to release and relax? Take a few moments to explore the dance of sensations in your body. There is no need to judge or control or change anything. Just open your awareness to this moment and these sensations in a simple act of noticing.

When you are ready to end your practice gently move your fingers and toes. Take a deep belly breath. And slowly release your posture.

You can take awareness breaks throughout the day by applying any aspects of this practice to connect with your breath and your body.

Chapter 2

Remembering to Pause and Attune

Quiet friend who has come so far, feel how your breathing makes more space around you.
—Rainer Maria Rilke

I used to view taking a pause as a lost opportunity for being productive. The art of slowing down to refuel or gain perspective was completely lost on me. I know I'm not alone. Many of us avoid pausing out of fear that we will lose momentum or control. And pausing means that we might have to feel our emotions, exhaustion or pain. We assume that it would be too much to handle if we stop and relax. So, we continue driving full speed down the highway of life and ignoring what we're experiencing on the inside.

My early diligence in practicing mindfulness helped me to recognize that driving full speed was not serving me well. Nor were my long hours of work or my tendency to ignore my basic needs. I knew that I had a choice of whether or not I wanted to continue living that way. But changing my habits wasn't that simple. I kept trying to bring mindfulness into the foreground of my days, but it would slip away like sand through my fingers. My meditation practice was consistent, but I would often find myself spinning out about the things I needed to accomplish or beating myself up about what wasn't going well when I was on the cushion. Off of my cushion, I would continue to mindlessly plow through life.

I recognized that I needed to build more intentional pauses into my day so I could be aware of my mental states and body. I took a few crucial steps that helped me to more regularly stop and attune. I began setting my alarm clock during the day to remind me to take intentional breaks. I would use that time for taking walks, mindful stretching or drinking tea. I also found a nearby yoga studio and built weekly classes into my schedule. The deep mental and somatic relief that I felt after class motivated me to begin a home yoga practice that would set the stage for my sitting meditation. Little by little, I became more deliberate about reminding myself to downshift with intentional pauses.

However, I didn't fully understand how powerful the pause could be until I experienced my first day-long meditation retreat, two years into my mindfulness journey. During the morning of the retreat, I found the sitting and walking practices difficult and had the impulse to jump up and run out the door more times than I could count. The friend who came with me on the retreat did run out the door. She had enough of her monkey mind by the time we were preparing for our silent lunch. But I stayed, observing the serene lead teacher with longing, seeing how the practice had settled deep within him, and returning to my breath a hundred times an hour. After lunch, settling back into sitting meditation, I touched into profound moments of quiet and peace. At one point, I simply disappeared. My breath was breathing, and a bird outside was singing, and they were connected in a beautiful way. In that moment, I felt fuller and emptier and more connected than I had in a very long time.

I stepped out of the meditation hall at the end of the retreat, back into my busyness, with a small but growing sense that I could access something larger than what my small-self had been revealing to me. I felt that there was something deeply stable within me that I could tap into at will. The day-long pause was an anomaly for me. At that point, I had a college teaching job that was demanding and stressful. But the day was a reminder of the gifts that presence can bestow when we give ourselves over to an elongated pause.

"Remembering" is one interpretation of Sati, the Pali word for mindfulness. In our quiet moments of connection with presence, our heart remembers who we are. Without establishing the habit of pausing and attuning, we can't experience what it is like to come home to ourselves or to access the calm that exists just below the waves. It is tricky to move toward mindfulness in a world that keeps us accelerating on the busy highway of life. How do we begin to notice and alter the habitual tendencies that keep us distracted from the present moment? The answer is simple but not easy to put into practice: we make the intention to slow down and attune to what is happening within and around us. We practice down-shifting gears and experience what it is like to stand still in the midst of it all. And we attend to what is happening with compassion and kindness. Bringing kind awareness to our resistance to pausing and attuning can help us recognize what stands in the way of presence. When we are ready to slow down, we can find our way to presence by taking a mindful stop and attuning internally.

The Bell of Mindfulness

Zen Master Thich Nhat Hanh describes mindfulness as "a bell that reminds us to stop and silently listen" (2015, p. 4). When we are moving down the road of life absentmindedly at warp speed, the simple reminder is to pause. But pausing is not simple. Consider this: how often do you pause during the day and notice what is going on? For many of us, the answer is "not very often." Now ask yourself: When is the last time you stopped for five minutes and did nothing but pay attention to your breath, or your body or how you were feeling inside? Many of us would say, "I can't remember."

Why is pausing so difficult? Our brains are not comfortable with stillness or not-doing. Our environments have been created to promote distraction. And our cultural conditioning has been directed toward productivity. Electronic devices have amplified our hardwiring toward doing. There is an addictive quality to staying busy. Our brains are not used to being still. As Kabat-

Zinn points out, we're really not human *beings*, we're human *doers*. When we are doing, we don't have to feel, acknowledge or accept what we don't like. Our busyness allows us to avoid our discomfort, unmet needs and unexamined anxieties and fears. Stopping to feel what is inside of us can be unfamiliar and uncomfortable.

So, slowing down is not easy. We need to re-train our brains how to do this. We need practice noticing our anxiety, reactivity and judgments. If we notice what is happening and sense the feelings we are covering up with noise and activity, we can change our trajectory by exploring what is coming up, with curiosity. We can get so carried away with our thoughts, fears and judgments that we fail to recognize that we don't have to be servants to our emotions. Instead, we can see our experiences for what they are—temporary states that come and go.

Once we stop and allow ourselves to settle, we can become aware of what is arising—a thought, emotion or sensation—and bring some objectivity to it rather than getting pulled into its energy or storyline. We do this by naming what we notice. This can be a neutral, objective label for what we see arising in the moment. We might say to ourselves—ah, there is worry or sadness or tightness in the shoulders. Our experience does not need to be labeled as good or bad. The worry, sadness or pain can be acknowledged as a momentary experience rather than a characteristic that defines us. From this more open and objective place, we can practice "being" with the feelings as they are, without making the good or bad.

Our practice helps us shift from seeing our experience as something that is happening *to* us to becoming a witness to what is happening *through* us. In other words, we recognize that our bodies are vehicles for our emotions and sensations that are constantly changing. When we can depersonalize the feelings or emotions, recognizing their transient nature, we find that we don't need to fear them, get attached to them or reject them. We don't need to do anything at all *about* them except to be with them, to the extent to which it is wise to do so.[4]

Our objectivity doesn't necessarily help to make difficult emotions feel any better or go away. In fact, our anxiety or fear might temporarily intensify when we notice it. But we become aware that our experience will change if we can pay attention to it. It might eventually dissipate when we take it out of the shadows and shine the light of awareness on it. Allowing the emotion or feeling to be what it is can be a powerful response rather than pushing it away. When we open space for the difficulty and take it out of the shadows, we find that the emotion tends to exert less power over us.

The Mindful STOP

We have to stop in order to attend to what is happening. The pause is the bridge between doing and being. Learning to stop is itself a practice. Sometimes we need structure for stopping. While I once used an alarm clock, we now have the benefit of phone apps and timers that can remind us to stop. But ultimately, we need self-permission and an appreciation for the value of the pause. There are times in our lives where we can't fit a meditation or yoga class into our schedule, or this formal approach doesn't interest us. But we can develop the habit of taking deliberate pauses.

There's a popular technique called the Mindful STOP that can be a powerful tool for getting started with the pause. It has four steps that I regularly share with my students when they are not sure how to approach making the pause part of their daily routine:

Stop: Cease what you are doing. Commit to taking a pause.

Take a few breaths: The breath can help us anchor in our body and bring us back to the present moment. If you are following the breath, your attention is focused in your body. And if your attention is in your body, you are by definition, present. You can simply notice the in-breath and out-breath as it rises and falls in your chest area. Or you can take deep diaphragmatic breaths, feeling your belly expanding on inhales and contracting on exhales. Bringing awareness to your breathing through any form of breathwork can help you bring your mind back to the body and the present moment.

Observe: Once you are present in your body, you can more easily attune to what is happening. As you let the awareness of your breathing fall to the background, you might do a quick scan of your body. Do you feel tension, heaviness or tingling? You might notice the area around your heart and the mood state that is present. Is there anger, sadness, fullness or joy? There is no need to judge what you find. This is information that you otherwise would not gather about yourself had you not intentionally slowed down. Just take a moment and observe what is going on internally. With this awareness, you are more able to identify what you need and what should happen next.

Proceed: When you have tuned into your breath and explored your body and its emotional states, you are in a much better position to decide how you want to proceed. Do you want to continue moving in the same direction you were heading before you began the Mindful STOP? Or is there a way to proceed that might better support you? This could be a walk or calling a friend. Or you might choose to pay attention to a bigger need like "I have to ask for help" or "I need to stop being so hard on myself." We have the ability to make wise choices that support our wellbeing rather than reacting thoughtlessly and even carelessly because we are not paying attention. Whatever choice you make is fine. There is no judgment here. What is important is that you recognize that you have a choice about what to do next.

Taking a pause or a Mindful STOP can allow us to step back, notice what is happening and be more thoughtful about how we want to be. It is not important how short or long the pause is. Any pause can be powerful. When you are more centered and present, you are more in touch with what you really need. The only prerequisite to the pause is a willingness to get still and feel. This willingness to touch into our inner world is courageous. And it is a powerful mediator for the habitual behaviors that often lead us toward avoidance, distraction, numbing and judging.

We can apply the strategies of pausing and attuning when a difficult emotion arises or when we recognize that we are feeling stuck. Rather than running away from our feelings, we are able to turn toward the difficulty and take a look. Over time, we can create new pathways in the brain that make it easier for us to pause and attune rather than reacting habitually out of discomfort. When we get trapped in feeling bad, depressed or anxious, initiating the pause can be difficult. In these cases, we may need to call on our supports to help us get unstuck. We can ask a friend or a partner to remind us to take a pause and perhaps get quiet together. We can listen to music or take a walk. We can seek out professional supports that can help create a safe space for us to name and allow what is happening. We can then begin to take the next step of befriending what shows up.

Meeting the Moment with Kindness

Tara Brach (2017) refers to Joseph Campbell's (1999) concept of the "Circle of Awareness" to demonstrate our inherent capacity for becoming more conscious of our everyday moments. We can imagine a circle with a horizontal line running through it. Everything above the line represents what is in our conscious awareness while everything below the line represents our unconscious. It is often the case that our line of awareness is at the top of the circle and a wide swath of our awareness is hidden below the line. We can intentionally move the line down through our practice of pausing and attuning. This image helps us to recognize that our line is not stuck in place; we are in control of what we choose to be aware of.

One way to wake up our awareness, Brach (2019) suggests, is that we ask ourselves: What is happening *in this moment*? I might notice that I'm feeling anxious about an upcoming meeting, or I am feeling anger toward my partner. Often, we bring judgment to what we notice—the anger turns into blame, or the anxiety becomes shame. Our awareness, *in the moment*, can help us see what is going on without getting caught in the story. Our attention is only focused on what is happening right now. This means that we don't need to project what will happen in the future. We don't have to add a layer of shame and blame. It can be incredibly freeing to just attend to what is happening in this moment.

When we see what is happening, we might then ask ourselves: Can I bring friendliness to what I'm experiencing *right now*? Or we might ask: How can I be with what is happening with kindness and care? Rather than judging or running away from something we don't like, we can put our hand on our heart and open space for the hurt, fear or whatever is arising. We can open to the moment with compassion.

It's not enough to attune to our feelings if we are harsh and judgmental toward ourselves and what we find. We must also bring kindness to whatever we feel. The two wings of mindfulness—awareness and compassion—are complementary. Paying attention to what is happening can wake up compassion if we are willing to let it open our hearts. And the softening of our hearts can further wake up our attention. With kindness our attention will grow. Awareness and compassion are two sides of the same mindfulness coin.

Mindfulness is often referred to as "heartfulness" because it is a practice that brings us closer to knowing and responding from our hearts. In fact, the Chinese calligraphy character for mindfulness is "present heart." With a present heart that is available and open, we can learn to bring care to ourselves when the waves get turbulent. Strengthening the wings of awareness and compassion, we have the ability to meet more of what life has to offer—both the joys and the sorrows—with greater courage and equanimity. When we learn to pause and cultivate a "present heart," we can be of greater service to ourselves and others.

Informal and Formal Practice

We can practice our Mindful STOP and cultivate "heartfulness" both when we are sitting on our cushion and when we are waiting at a stop light or watching our child's soccer practice. Both the *informal* and *formal* practice of bringing mindful awareness and compassion to the moment are critical for deepening mindfulness.

There are a few issues to unpack about formal meditation practice. First, meditation doesn't only take place when we are doing seated meditation. Our meditation practice can take many forms, from standing meditation to body scan to walking meditation. What makes the practice "formal" is that it is the only activity that is being done at that time. When we meditate, we bring an intention to steady the mind, open our awareness and stay with what is happening. So, if we have an impulse to check our phone while doing sitting meditation, we notice and acknowledge that impulse, bring curiosity to it and maybe even offer compassion to ourselves for wanting to flee the moment. Our commitment in formal meditation is to remain present and anchored in our moment-to-moment awareness. That is the only thing we are doing.

However, we don't need to be formally sitting, walking or doing a body scan meditation to bring mindfulness into our moment. Informal practice means that we're bringing mindful awareness to the activities we perform. We might be walking our dog *and* noticing our breath. We may be washing the dishes *and* bringing awareness to our hands. We might be in the middle of a challenging phone call *and* noticing the feeling of frustration arising. We can listen mindfully, paying close attention to the words, energy and body language of the person we are listening to. We can drive mindfully, swim mindfully and listen to music mindfully.

According to Shapiro and Carlson, these "little m" practices help us build the "Big M" of Mindful Awareness which is "fundamentally a way of being – a way of inhabiting one's body, one's mind, one's moment-by-moment experience" (2009, p. 5). Both our formal meditation and informal practices are vehicles for the cultivation of Mindful Awareness. As this awareness grows and strengthens, our meditation practice often becomes richer and deeper. And as our meditation practice becomes deeper, so too does our capacity for attention, concentration and compassion.

We often assume that unless we are formally meditating, we aren't strengthening our mindfulness. While formal meditation practice is a powerful and important tool for building concentration and deepening our awareness, our mindfulness can be strengthened through all sorts of "little m" applications in our everyday lives. Both facets of our practice are important. The key to growing our capacity for mindfulness is our intention. We can come to understand that the seeds we water are the ones that will grow.

Some Fundamentals of Formal Meditation Practice

There is a common Hindu proverb that says, "There are hundreds of paths up the mountain, all leading to the same place, so it doesn't matter which path you take. The only person wasting time is the one who runs around the mountain, telling everyone that his or her path is wrong." So too does this proverb apply to mindfulness meditation, our formal practice. When you are ready to develop a formal meditation practice, keep in mind that there is no right or wrong way to practice, but there are some general principles to take into consideration.

Find Your Space and Time

If you want to commit to a regular practice, then find a space in your house that allows you the best chance at the fewest distractions possible. This probably won't be in the middle of your living room unless you live alone. Perhaps it is a quiet corner of your bedroom or in a study. Choose a regular time of the day to practice. You may need to communicate with your family or roommates that you will be practicing then and ask to not be interrupted. Figure out what you need to succeed at a regular daily practice. Perhaps start with a commitment to a short practice (like 5–10 minutes a day). Only increase your practice time when the habit has taken hold and you've gained confidence. What is important is the consistency of your practice, not the length of time.

Find Your Posture

You don't have to sit on the floor cross-legged to meditate. Your practice can be far simpler than that. Find a chair or a couch or a cushion to sit on. You may want to follow advice given by Bhante Henepola Gunaratana in *Mindfulness in Plain English*: "Your spine should be like a firm young tree growing out of the soft ground. The rest of the body just hangs from it in a loose, relaxed manner" (2011, p. 58). A straight spine will help you concentrate. If you are sitting on a chair, feeling your feet planted firmly on the ground can help you feel rooted and supported by the earth. You might place your hands gently in your lap either facing up or down. Your position should be both alert and relaxed. You can close your eyes or place your gaze softly a foot or two in front of you. Feel the dignity and strength of your seated position.

Find an Anchor

The breath can be a wonderful anchor that you can return to whenever your mind wanders. Notice where your attention most naturally rests when you breathe. That might be on your nostrils where you feel the cool air coming in and warm air going out. You might naturally place your attention on your chest rising and falling with the in-breath and out-breath. Or your attention might gravitate to your belly as it expands and contracts. Once you find that natural resting place for your attention, practice following your breath as it breathes naturally. If you need a stronger anchor to hold your attention, you might silently note "breathing in, breathing out" or you might count to four or five as you breathe in and out. If the breath doesn't feel like a good anchor, you might consider allowing the sensations of your hands or feet to serve as an anchor. Or allow sounds to be your anchor. The majority of your attention can rest on your anchor and when you find your mind wandering or you get distracted, you can notice what is happening, name it ("distraction" or "thinking") and come back to your anchor... again and again.

Set Appropriate Expectations

Learning to quiet the mind and develop concentration doesn't happen overnight. So, it's useful to let go of any goals for your practice. Don't expect anything to happen. Meditation should not be undertaken as a self-improvement project. This will only set up unnecessary expectations that will lead to striving (future-focused attention) and self-judgment (negativity). Changes may or may not come about. If they do, they certainly won't happen within the timeframe that you would like. So, it is important to practice for the sake of practicing. As Larry Rosenberg writes, "The deepest paradox in all of meditation: we want to get somewhere—we wouldn't have taken up the practice if we didn't—but the way to get there is just to be fully here. The way to get from point A to point B is really to be at A. When we follow the breathing in the hope of becoming something better, we are compromising our connection to the present, which is all we ever have" (2004, p. 33).

Take Care of Your Body

Many of us are not used to sitting still. As much as this can be difficult for our minds, it can also be hard on our bodies. We might strain our backs or find that our legs fall asleep easily. It is worth bringing mindful awareness to these discomforts without immediately trying to resolve them. However, we need to find a balance between good effort in our practice and taking care of ourselves. If you are meditating, don't strain in an uncomfortable position beyond the point of it being healthy or helpful (you will need to learn how to determine that). Move slowly and deliberately to change position when it is time. And be kind to yourself if you find that your body aches more than you would like.

Be Prepared to Allow Distractions

As soon as you sit down to practice, the dog will inevitably start barking, the construction workers next door will begin hammering or the kids will barge in. If those external distractions don't happen, there will surely be a range of internal noises, thoughts and fantasies to take your mind away from your anchor. Be open to these distractions and let them into your practice. Instead of wishing them away, you can welcome them. Say, "Okay, here's the dog and he is part of my practice today" or "Here's the garbage truck and I will allow these sounds into my practice." There really is no such thing as a distraction if you're willing to be open to whatever is happening.

Learn to Stay

Thoughts will arise along with discomfort, pain, sleepiness, boredom, irritation and ten thousand other distractions. With a light touch, notice what is arising, without getting pulled into its storyline. You can name what is happening ("pain," "sleepiness," "boredom") and explore it with curiosity. No need to get pulled into its energy, judge or reject what is happening. Just practice letting the experience be as it is. Eventually it will change, and the next thought or impulse will come up. You can watch the sensation for a little while. And when you are ready, you can return to your anchor and the present moment. If your impulse is to get off the chair or cushion, see if you can wait out that impulse and settle back in at least two more times. Give yourself the chance to be uncomfortable and impatient. Let those impulses and your resistance to the practice become your focus for a short while. And then return to your anchor.

Accept What Arises

You can't control the thoughts that will come into your head or the feelings in your heart or the aches in your body. You may not like a lot of it. But whatever is happening is happening. You can hang out your welcome mat to the good, bad and ugly experiences. They all have something to teach us. When we can open with curiosity and accept what is arising, we often find that things are more workable than we initially thought. We can make space for the experience to arise and then unhand the experience, sensation, thought or emotion... watching it move out of sight like a cloud in the sky.

Know Your Limits

It's important to use wise discernment in your practice. If you feel your anxiety rising to an alarming level or a traumatic memory playing out in your mind, you should not push through it. You might shift your attention back and forth from the discomfort (e.g., feeling of anxiety) to a more neutral place in your body (like your hands or feet). You might picture in your mind a caring being who showers you with love. Or you might try walking meditation—taking slow, purposeful steps and paying attention to the sensations in your feet—which can be very grounding. But it is okay to abandon the practice. Meditation is not suitable for everyone or under every circumstance. Nor is it a "cure-all" for our distress. If you are distressed, then you need to take care of yourself. There are times when we need other forms of self-care or professional support rather than meditation.

The Mindful Reframe

By now it should be apparent that as we sit on our cushion, we are not always met with perfect peace. The Zen-mind of our cartoon dog in Chapter 1 is not often available to us. Instead, we find that our monkey mind and habits of grasping and aversion go into overdrive. What we've been avoiding, distracting from or unwilling to feel might show up in our practice. Or we may get bored or feel dull, numb and flat. With peace alluding us, we might jump to the conclusion that we are not doing meditation right.

We tend to bring this dualistic view to our practice: if I'm feeling peaceful, I'm doing it right and if I'm not, I'm doing it wrong. But we can learn over time that this is a false dichotomy. We are not seeking "peace" or trying to make things better; we aren't trying to eliminate the bad stuff and find our way toward happiness. We are simply becoming aware and learning to lean into the discomforts rather than making them our enemy. As Mingyur Rinpoche writes, "We want smooth ocean waters with no waves. When the waves come, we say we cannot meditate; or we assume that the presence of waves means we are not meditating correctly. But the waves keep coming anyway, always. It is how we perceive them that changes" (2019, p. 43).

Mindfulness is about being in wise relationship with our experiences. This implies that we don't turn our experiences into the enemy. We can learn instead to meet them with curiosity. As the Sufi poet Rumi writes in "The Guest House": "The dark thought, the shame, the malice. Meet them at the door laughing and invite them in. Be grateful for whatever comes because each has been sent as a guide from beyond." I often suggest to my students that when a difficult thought or emotion arises, imagine inviting it to sit down with you for a cup of tea. It's always interesting what can happen when we take a deep look into the eyes of our anger or anxiety.

When we are willing to pause, we have greater ability to notice, name and allow what is happening. As we move our line of awareness down the circle, we can begin to see more clearly what is distracting us from the present moment. As we become more familiar with our inner landscape, we come to recognize that a thought is just a thought, an emotion is just an emotion and a story is just a story; when we don't get hooked by these things, we can see their fleeting nature. Our moment-by-moment experience becomes less layered with reactivity and judgment. As we will see in the next chapter, our capacity to pause and attune can help us respond rather than react when the inevitable life stressors come to visit us. Rather than shoving them out the door, we can invite them for tea and listen to what they have to say.

***

Practice: Remembering to Pause

Learning how to make the pause a regular part of your day is a practice. It requires intention and commitment. Take this moment to consider how would you like to bring more pauses into your days, reflecting on the steps of the Mindful STOP. Once you have established your plan, take a pause and try it out!

Stop: How would you like to integrate Mindful STOPs during the day? You might want to incorporate some time for breathwork, take a tea break, do some stretching or mindfully walk. What would your "pause" schedule look like? How much time would you invest in your pauses? What tools, devices or reminders would be most helpful for ensuring that you follow through on these regular pauses?

If you would like to develop a regular formal meditation practice, consider what that would look like. When would you regularly practice? Where would you find a quiet space with minimal interruptions? What barriers might you need to address in order to make this work? Whether you choose to start a formal practice and/or desire more "mindful moments" throughout the day, take a moment to envision how you would like to feel after you take your pause. Specifically, what does your body feel like? What does it feel like to have settled your mind?

Take a Breath: Consider now the role that your awareness of breath will play in your formal practice and/or mindful moments. Your breath is a wonderful gateway to your body and to the present moment. To establish a connection with your breath, you might begin your pause with a few deep belly breaths. Notice how your belly naturally expands on a deep inhale and contracts on the exhale. Perhaps take three deep diaphragmatic breaths once you have paused. If you find it more helpful to focus your mind through counting, the simple box breath is a good starting point. This involves inhaling for a count of four, holding for a count of four, exhaling for a count of four and holding for a count of four. You may find that four repetitions of the box breath help to establish your focus.

Once you complete your diaphragmatic or box breaths, let go of your focus on your belly or on the counting and let your breathing happen naturally. Gently rest your awareness on the in- and out-breath. When you find that your mind has wandered, return your attention back to your breath, your anchor in the present moment.

Observe: This is your moment for attuning. Let the breath awareness fall to the background and take a moment to scan your body with interest and kind attention. What do you notice? What is calling your attention? You might tune into your heart space. What emotions are present? There is no need to analyze or think about anything you are discovering. This part of the practice is simply for recognizing and allowing what is present for you in this moment.

Proceed: Once you have completed these three steps, take a moment to consider what will serve you best moving forward. How would you like to proceed now that you slowed things down? There is no right or wrong answer. What is important is that you have given yourself the choice.

Chapter 3

Relaxing Our Reactivity

Between stimulus and response there is a space. In that space is our power to choose our response. In our response lies our growth and our freedom.
—Viktor Frankl

Many of us are initially drawn to mindfulness because we are looking for stress relief. We may feel overwhelmed by life's demands, responsibilities and hardships. We may long to slow down, experience what it is like to relax and feel better. When we begin meditating, we may feel frustrated that it's not easy to turn down the noise volume and release the tension we are carrying. Our distractions, discomforts and agitations can surprise us as we try to sit still. We may experience disillusionment that we can't "meditate away" our difficulties. The hard truth that we encounter is that the only way around our discomfort is through it. If we are willing to pause and listen, we can find that the stressors in our lives offer opportunities to learn how to respond rather than react to the difficulties we face.

Many years ago, this lesson presented itself to me in the form of a book manuscript rejection. I came home one Friday afternoon from an acupuncture appointment feeling a deep sense of calm; my nervous system had been soothed and my mind quieted. I felt so good that I decided I was going to take the weekend off from grading papers and suggest a spontaneous road trip to Brendon when he came home from work. But then the email came. A book proposal that I had submitted a few months prior had been rejected. The publisher thanked me for the submission and explained that my project was not ready for prime time. I immediately felt the fires of rejection ignite in my body. The burning of failure, the frustration of time lost and the familiar story of "not good enough" took hold. The ease and hopefulness I had felt a few moments prior immediately vanished. Weekend plans were dropped before they ever left my lips.

I watched myself dissolve into despair that weekend. First rage, then self-judgment, then helplessness. Part of me was confused by what seemed like an oversized reaction to this rejection. My angst about the book did not match where I thought I was in my mindfulness practice. I assumed I was farther along in embodying the qualities that I had been actively practicing for a few years at that point, particularly non-striving, patience, trust and acceptance. Questions washed over me as I sat with the burning rejection. Why was I still so identified with my accomplishments? Where was this internal pressure coming from? How could I release my attachment and reactivity? What did I need to let go of?

My meditation practice that weekend allowed me to pause and calm my reactivity, rebalance my nervous system and bring my rational mind back online. I was able to put things into perspective by reconnecting with my core, stable self. In doing so, I recognized that it was time to explore these questions more deeply with the support of a therapist. Over the next few months, I acknowledged out loud for the first time how critical and harsh I was on myself and how my self-induced pressures were a barrier to the freedom that I knew was possible. My therapist held space for what became a profound process of "undoing" and releasing my attachments to an identity that was profoundly constricting. And my mindfulness practice held me steady, and still does, when I revert back to my small, fearful self.

Our reactivity to life's curve balls and stressors can distract us from what lies underneath the pain. This could include a legacy of unmet needs, a sense of unworthiness or a fear of being unlovable. When reactivity goes unexamined, we can solidify protective behaviors and miss the signals that stressors offer to direct us toward seeing things more clearly. Bringing awareness to these pivotal moments by practicing mindfulness can help us see when our stressors are valuable gifts, rather than obstacles in our way.

Our Constant Companion

Stress can be a constant companion for many of us. The busyness, noise and speed of our lives has rapidly accelerated over the last decades. We face different stressors based on our life stage and circumstances as we seek meaningful work, balance family and work life, care for our kids and aging parents and accept care as we age. We inevitably experience crises on top of our daily stressors like illness, financial hardship, divorce, natural disasters and pandemics (or all of the above which has, sadly, become possible). Whether the difficulty is moderate or massive in scope, short-term or chronic, stress can generate a number of psychological and physiological symptoms like anxiety, fear, depression and fatigue. Stress can force the "on button" of our activated nervous system to get jammed, keeping us in a perpetual state of fight or flight.

Stress is considered "endemic" in our society as it has a deep and wide reach. Prior to the pandemic, stress had already reached epidemic levels in our society. According to the American Institute of Stress, between 75–90% of visits to primary health care providers occurred on account of stress-related symptoms. The American Psychological Association's 2019 Stress in America survey showed that more than three-quarters of adults reported physical or emotional symptoms of stress, such as headaches, feeling tired or changes in sleeping habits. Nearly half of adults said they had laid awake at night because of stress the prior month. The pandemic and ensuing conflicts have added a significant burden of stress. The 2022

Stress in America survey found that over half of Americans needed more emotional support than they were receiving.

The expression of stress plays out differently for different people and in different circumstances, but it inevitably impacts many areas of our lives. When we feel overwhelmed, we may isolate and withdraw from our natural sources of support. We may invest less time in leisure activities which can lead to more isolation and sedentary behavior. And anyone who has ever tossed and turned after a difficult day knows that stress can make it hard to sleep well. While media overload may contribute to our stress and insomnia, we might still turn on the TV or scroll through social media to soothe our nocturnal discomfort.

Our health providers tell us to exercise, sleep better and eat more balanced meals when we're stressed. But when psychological states of worry, anxiety or depression fuel the fire of stress, we may not be motivated to follow "expert" advice. Our short-term habits of seeking relief from stress may come in the form of comfort eating, numbing with alcohol or other substances or technology addiction. The desire for relief may override our rational awareness of or motivation for health-promoting behaviors, and we may find ourselves aggravating our stress with our coping behaviors, rather than relieving it.

Since we live in a culture that tends to medicalize emotional struggles, it is not often that our health provider will encourage us to bring awareness to our discomfort around the stress, explore it and see what it might be telling us, rather than or in addition to taking a pill to fix it. We are not often told that we might *non-judgmentally* explore the conditions causing stress to see if there are steps we can take to decrease our suffering. We certainly don't learn to notice our reactivity to our stress or understand how to prevent a trigger from becoming an emotional or behavioral storm. It is often overlooked that mindful *awareness* — the thing we often strive so hard to avoid — is in fact a starting point for stress relief and resilience. But if we look closely, we can see that mindfulness, in fact, can contain the seeds of relief for our discomfort.

How We Experience Stress

We often think of stress as coming from outside of us—from the external circumstances we face and the difficulties we encounter. This is certainly the case as external stressors can be acute such as illness, poverty and social and racial inequalities. Yet, much of our stress is generated and amplified internally. For example, we fear failure, so we activate our perfectionist tendencies which hampers success and creates depression, anxiety, addiction and life paralysis (Brown, 2010). Or we fear loneliness, so we react by withdrawing which exacerbates our experience of social isolation.

There are many sources that drive our internal stressors including familial messages that we internalize, societal pressures that we adopt and even generational and genetic trauma that we inherit. Trauma from our past—both large and small experiences—can burrow into our minds and bodies. Stored trauma, which can result in a number of symptoms that range in severity, can be difficult to extract and it is masterful at amplifying our reactivity. The nervous system holds onto trauma, causing deep suffering in our minds, hearts and lives.

In moments of stress and when we get activated, our natural instinct might be to turn away from others, self-protect and distract from difficult emotions. We might become self-consumed. Our world may become small and narrow as we zone in on our personal suffering. Perhaps we don't notice how on edge we are because it is not comfortable to slow down and look inside. It may be only when an external crisis directly strikes—like a diagnosis or a breakup that we pull ourselves to attention, notice what is happening and seek help. But whether or not we are aware, our bodies and minds know what is happening. The alarm bells start ringing because we are hardwired with a very ancient warning system that has developed to keep us safe. When we experience stress:

- Stress hormones are released
- The body gets tense
- The mind gets constricted
- We shift into a "fight-or-flight" reaction or we go into "freeze" mode

Our brains and bodies know what to do to keep us safe as they did thousands of years ago when we occupied the savannah alongside hungry tigers. Our amygdala gets activated and fear signals are sent through our bodies warning us to prepare for action. The sympathetic nervous system (SNS) triggers the secretion of stress hormones like adrenaline and cortisol. Our heartrate and breathing speed up. Our muscles get tense and strong. We prepare for action in body and mind. These natural, built-in physiological reactions to stress help to explain why humans have survived for so long.

Our SNS is part of our body's great evolutionary intelligence. It is helpful when we need to flee to protect ourselves or fight our way out of a dangerous situation. But sometimes our bodies stay stuck in fight-or-flight mode for a long time. When the chronic stress of our modern lifestyles, difficult circumstances or unresolved trauma are not abated, our SNS may stay activated. This state not only takes a toll on our bodies, but it can create chronic anxiety and depression, which reinforces our stress state.

We have a built-in brake mechanism for the SNS. The parasympathetic nervous system (PNS) is what allows us to "rest and digest." It has the opposite job of the sympathetic nervous system. Rather than revving us up for action, the PNS helps us quiet and calm down. It decreases our respiration and heart rate and increases digestion. We have the capacity to activate our PNS when we are stressed. And we can step on the brakes of the SNS and slow the activation train down. We need our parasympathetic and sympathetic nervous systems to work in balance with each other, kind of like the gas pedal and brakes of a car. And we need to understand how to do this.

The Relaxation Response

Basic breathing techniques are a good starting point for bringing the SNS and PNS into balance. We may hear about breathing techniques and not give them much thought. Or we may think, "I've got the breathing thing down. I do it all the time." While this is true, we don't often breathe consciously, in a way that can support our nervous system. In fact, we tend to breathe short, shallow breaths from our upper chest. We do not often stop to take deep full breaths from our belly which can offer benefits like slowing our heart rate, increasing the oxygen that enters our blood stream and sending messages to our brain to relax.

The breath is interesting on another level. Breathing is at the intersection of the body, the conscious mind and the unconscious mind. When you don't think about breathing, you are able to do it unconsciously, thanks to the autonomic nervous system (ANS) that functions independent from the conscious mind. But we can influence the breath consciously which allows us to have power over the mind. The way in which we choose to breathe can direct the ANS; we can influence whether we speed up our fight-or-flight reaction or we slow it down by activating the PNS.

Deep, slow, diaphragmatic breathing is one simple way to balance our nervous system. A deep belly breath has the effect of downregulating the nervous system whereas shallow chest breathing has the opposite effect. A good way to consciously breathe is by placing one hand on your belly so you can feel your belly expanding on the inhale and contracting on the exhale. You might put the other hand on your chest to make sure you're not breathing short, shallow breaths from your chest. Practice doing a deep belly breath by breathing in through your nose and exhaling through your mouth (this slows the flow of air down). Perhaps when you breathe out, put the tip of your tongue on the roof of your mouth (just behind your front teeth), let your lips relax and slowly let the air escape around your tongue. This will further slow down the air as it exits your mouth.

If you read the last paragraph in its entirety, you probably have already slowed down your breathing. Your body instinctively knows what to do. It's like the reflex you get when you see someone laugh—you at least find yourself smiling. In this case, just reading about deep breathing activates our PNS. The conscious act of taking a breath or two initiates a pause in our mental activity. This can be our starting point when we feel tension rising or begin to feel stressed.

Diaphragmatic (belly) breathing relieves muscle tension, releases natural waste and increases oxygen to cells. It can calm and center you right there on the spot. At any given moment you can change the direction of your autonomic nervous response. You can practice belly breathing in your car at stop lights, during stressful phone calls, at the doctor's office, as well as during quiet moments at home or before you go to sleep. My family takes three deep breaths together before eating dinner. The breath is a wonderful way to drop any drama going on in your head. It moves you into your body, which is the best way to return to the present moment.

Diaphragmatic breathing is not the only technique available to us. There are countless ways we utilize conscious breathing to put on the SNS brakes. The box breath that we explored in the practice at the end of the last chapter and other coherence breathing strategies are just as easy to do as the diaphragmatic breath. Coherent breathing techniques are beneficial because they enact slow, deep breathing in which you inhale and exhale for the same amount of time with pauses in between. The technique increases the activity of the vagus nerve, a part of the PNS which activates calmness, slows and regulates heart rate, decreases blood pressure and causes muscles to relax (André, 2019).

Breathing techniques are one category of accessible practices that we can use to moderate our stress in the moment. They are always available to us, don't cost a penny and require a limited amount of time and effort. Our meditation practices, where we consciously follow the breath or thoughts or sensations, also help us balance our nervous system. The mindfulness required to do breathing practices, sitting meditation, walking meditation or a body scan can help us moderate the fight-or-flight reaction to stress. These practices move our attention away from our scattered, agitated mind and focus it on our body, breath or feet, helping us ground and center. Our attention on the body is a tool for getting present. And getting present—rather than catastrophizing the future or worrying about the past—is helpful for regulating stress.

Meditation practitioners have known this for thousands of years. Research that accompanied the rise of Western interest in meditation gave a name to this. Herbert Benson first coined the phrase "relaxation response" in the 1970s. Research shows that we can encourage our bodies to release chemicals and brain signals that create a slowing down and calming effect. Breathing techniques and mindfulness meditation are not the only tools we can use to achieve nervous system balance. Practices like yoga, tai-chi, qi gong, progressive relaxation and even prayer can initiate the relaxation response and stimulate the PNS. Learning deep relaxation techniques can help us lower our stress level, reduce blood pressure, strengthen our immune system and lift our mood.

How We Respond to Stress

We can be proactive about balancing our nervous system and calming our fight-or-flight reaction. The actions we take—like conscious breathing and meditation—are deeply supportive. Their regular use over time helps us rewire our neuronal circuitry and allows for a quicker return to balance after we get activated, as will be discussed in the next chapter. However, the way we perceive stress and respond to it with awareness is equally important. We need to understand the difference between a reaction and a response and how we naturally perpetuate stress in order to fully understand the possibilities for mindfully managing stress.

When we *react*, we are immediately flung into a heightened emotional state. We might get triggered by something—a phone call, an interaction, a bill—and our stress level shoots from a zero to ten in a matter of a few seconds. We might react with anger, aggression or fear, or we could withdraw or isolate. These are habituated, protective responses that we have relied upon throughout the course of our lives. A reaction happens when there is no pause between a trigger and our next action. Without a pause, our emotions get free range. There is no buffer. And the result is that we may say or do things that do not come from our rational brains. These might be things that we later regret.

If we build a pause between the trigger and what happens next, we are more likely to *respond* rather than react. Because of the pause or break in the situation, we have an opportunity to *choose* to do something different than react in our habituated way. We may take a breath, call a time out or walk away from a heated situation. Depending how far we are into our reaction, our pause might need to last a while. I took a multi-day pause after my book rejection to settle my nervous system and gain perspective. Learning to build in the appropriate amount of space to respond to difficult moments is a skill that requires mindfulness.

Our ability to respond rather than react benefits from noticing what is happening as close to the moment of trigger as possible. Once emotions get stirred up, it becomes more difficult to initiate a pause. When we slow things down, we can more easily tune into the sensations or emotions that are arising in our body. Slowing down can prevent us from getting swept up into the waves of emotions. Bringing mindful awareness to the moment helps our rational brains come back online.

The sensation that tends to alert me to a trigger has long been a feeling of adrenaline, particularly in my legs. When I get triggered in an upsetting conversation or situation, I tend to experience a palpable rising of energy in my legs. Over the years, I've learned to notice when the adrenaline begins to rise. That has become a signal to me that my sympathetic nervous system is shifting out of balance. I now take conscious breaths or send myself some compassion when I notice the signal. If I'm in the middle of a heated discussion, I might take a pause or break, and examine exactly what I am feeling. This has taken me years of practice, but I have built confidence over time that I have the ability to shift my reactivity, rather than letting my reactions be in control.

We learn through our mindfulness practice that what happens within us when we get upset is not to be feared; it can be explored and welcomed as our body's intelligent way of communicating. We so often override our feelings, emotions or sensations and react from a place of anger or fear, forgetting to listen to the body's intelligence. When we can bring an open curiosity to our experience, we can hear the messages we are being given. We can respond more wisely, rather than reacting harshly, in any given situation.

How We Decrease Our Suffering

We may not realize how much we fuel the fires of our stress until the harmful consequences of our actions—toward ourselves and others—are brought to light. When we assume our partner has intentionally left a towel on the floor for us to trip over, we lash out in anger. The minute it turns 10 p.m. and our teenage child hasn't come home, we catastrophize car crash stories. When we fixate on our anger or fear stories, we exacerbate our stress. Put simply, we suffer when we add fuel to the fire.

There's a saying used often in mindfulness teachings: Pain is inevitable, suffering is optional. Our reaction to the inevitable pain in our lives amplifies our suffering. Here is a formula that shows how this works:

Suffering = Pain × Reaction or Resistance

The "pain" in the formula is the initial difficulty: the job furlough, the air conditioner quitting, the fender bender, the book rejection. These are painful things. And they will naturally elicit an emotional reaction. But this formula suggests that the extent to which we suffer is directly related to the extent to which we react to or resist what is happening.

Our reactions are considered "second arrows"—the arrows we continue to throw after the initial arrow of pain comes our way. For example, my book rejection email arrives. The initial arrow is cast. I fall into despair and self-judgment saying to myself "I knew my work wasn't good enough." I've thrown a second arrow. I drop plans for what might have been a rejuvenating weekend. The third arrow is cast. I might have even irrationally blamed Brendon for involving me in activities that took away time from perfecting the book. The arrows can go on and on. Some of the arrows are self-directed while others might be aimed at others. There are a million ways we react to or resist what we don't like. When we react by throwing arrows, our suffering increases as does the suffering of those who are standing in the line of fire.

What is an alternative? We can turn our awareness to what is happening in the moment. We can investigate what is coming up, not from our analytic mind but from our witness state. When we bring awareness to the stories, feelings and emotions, with gentleness and without judgment, we can see that what we are experiencing is *real* but not *true* (Brach, 2016). It is real in the sense that we experience the anger or frustration as a contraction of our body or mind. But it is not true because the anger or frustration is just a passing reaction, coming from a story that we tell ourselves about the way things should be.

When we become curious and aware, we might recognize the agitations for what they are—passing, temporary, fleeting thoughts, feelings and sensations. If we are willing to take the seat of the witness and watch what is happening, we will see that the reactivity will eventually pass, even the stickiest experiences of fear and anger. And if we are willing to acknowledge the temporary nature of these experiences and let go of their hold on us, then we can be freed to receive a larger perspective. Letting go can't be forced. It may take a lot of time for a story or emotion to loosen its grip. But the intention to let go is a very compassionate response to the stress in our lives.

Stress doesn't only happen on account of external circumstances. We create a lot of disturbance on our own. We can create emotional waves that are intense and even violent. But if we allow ourselves to pause and look closely, we might find that under the surface exists a quiet, gentle body of water. This describes our minds—both the waves and what lies below the surface—and we have a choice about which level to inhabit.

Staying Steady in the Moment

Stress is by no means a terrible thing. We are motivated by stress. It pushes us to take action, get out of harm's way, make positive changes and continue growing. There is such a thing as "eustress," which is positive stress that occurs on account of making a job change, falling in love, raising a child or writing a book. Our bodies and minds get "activated," but in a good way. It is when we make stress our enemy and we are not able to put the brakes on the SNS that we find ourselves out of balance, overwhelmed and anxious.

One benefit of our mindfulness practice is that it helps us decrease the lag time between getting triggered and noticing what is happening. When we are aware that we are getting activated, we can make the choice to slow down, open up space for what is happening, and lean into, rather than running away from, our discomfort and difficulty. We can learn that we have a choice in how to respond.

While we may not have much control over our external circumstances — the pandemic and many recent natural disasters reinforce this truth — we do have control over how we respond. As Holocaust survivor Viktor Frankl writes: "When we are no longer able to change a situation, we are challenged to change ourselves." As much as we might try, we can't avoid distress and discomfort. But our mindfulness practice can help us learn how to right-size our *reaction* to stress, widen the lens through which we view our difficulties and choose the most appropriate action. So, while the conditions that produce stress may not be within our control, our response to stress can be.

When we react to stress with fear, aversion and hostility, we create added layers of suffering for ourselves and for others. Our stress reactivity and arrow-throwing can block us from recognizing the freedom that is available to us. It can also prevent us from living our lives in alignment with our true selves. The reverse of this is true. When we are leading from our core selves, meeting our stress with mindfulness can be a "curriculum for transformation," as the late meditation teacher Ram Das describes it.

In my case, a book rejection became an opportunity for radical transformation. My path of "undoing" has led me to discover a deeper awareness of and appreciation for who I am, without prerequisites or conditions. The painful moment of rejection helped me to see the cage that I had constructed for myself. As I have learned to work mindfully with the difficulties in my life, I have been able to move toward a far more gentle, kind and compassionate relationship with myself than I ever knew was possible.

Interestingly, an unexpected invitation arrived after I had let go of my painful attachment to publishing my book. Three months after the rejection arrived in my in-box, I was approached at a conference by an editor for a university press who was interested in what I had just presented. "Do you think you might ever want to turn your research into a book?" she asked. I couldn't help but laugh. "It just so happens..." I responded as I took a breath and began an entirely new relationship with the project. It can be surprising what happens when we relate differently to our circumstances. And as we will see in the next chapter, how we choose to direct our thoughts, mindfully, can make all the difference.

***

Practice: Relaxing Our Nervous System

This is a gentle practice of letting go of tension that arises in your mind and body as you get triggered or reactive.

You can begin this practice by taking a few moments to focus on the breath. You might choose to close your eyes or to keep the eyes open, with a soft downward gaze. Notice your posture and see if you can settle into an alert but relaxed position on your chair or cushion. Now, bring your attention to your breath as it naturally rises and falls in your chest or your belly. If you find it difficult to "anchor" in your breath, you might choose instead to place your attention on the sensations in your hands or your feet. Whichever anchor you choose, just focus your attention gently on the anchor and let it be the gateway into your body awareness and the present moment.

You might let the awareness of breathing or sensations fall to the background and shift your attention to your body as you do a gentle body scan. Open your awareness to whatever sensations become present as you sweep your attention slowly from the top of your head down your neck, through your shoulders back, belly, pelvis, legs and feet. You are simply feeling your body from the inside out, not trying to make anything happen. As you do your body scan, notice if you can detect any tension or tightness or if there is discernible anxiety.

If you detect tension or anxiety, place your attention wherever you feel it in your body and notice if you can imagine the tension melting like ice. If you are having difficulty imagining the melting, try breathing in and out through this particular area of your body, bringing kindness and tenderness to the tension or anxiety. You might imagine whispering to the tension, "Thank you for trying to protect me. I'm okay now."

Then continue the body scan, placing your attention on the areas of your body in which you detect tension or anxiety. Notice if there can be a melting or a softening as you gently breathe in and out of the tension, bringing kindness and gratitude to it for trying to protect you.

In this practice, we turn our awareness toward the parts of the body that are expressing anxiety or reactivity with gentleness rather than judgment. When we open up space for the tension with kindness—breathing in and out of our body—we might find ourselves relaxing a little bit more. We can thank the tension or anxiety for protecting us, rather than pushing it away. In doing so, our nervous system has the chance to release and reset rather than continuing to be on guard and alert.

There is a difference between approaching this practice actively or passively. Sometimes, it is most helpful to intentionally relax the areas of tension in our body. However, there is sometimes more benefit to just letting the tension be there and staying with it in awareness. You can rotate between these approaches to see what works best for you.

Chapter 4

Redirecting Our Negativity

We all carry within us our places of exile, our crimes, our ravages. Our task is not to unleash them on the world; it is to transform them in ourselves and others.
—Albert Camus

George Mumford, a meditation teacher who has coached NBA greats, has pointed out: "You are not what you think you are; but what you think, you are."[5] Mindfulness makes us aware of how the narratives and stories that we create and strengthen in our minds can have significant influence in our lives and in the world. Our thoughts and words can be directed for the good. But the reverse can also be true. We can do a lot of harm with our unkind thoughts and words. We have a choice in what to think and believe, and how we choose to direct our minds fundamentally makes a difference.

I didn't fully understand my capacity for directing my mind—for better or for worse—until I found myself in the throes of parenthood. Despite the positive traction I had gained in my mindfulness practice, busyness and exhaustion took control of the reins after Aidan was born. At that point, my *real* "curriculum for transformation" was initiated; all previous lessons had been purely preparatory.

As I mentioned earlier, my mindfulness practice went out the door as soon as Aidan was born. The intensive caregiving that was required, along with a full-time job that I resumed after maternity leave, led me to experience pure exhaustion. I cherished my moments with Aidan, but I found myself overwhelmed and depressed and I experienced profound guilt and shame for having those feelings. I would see other parents happily playing with their kids at the park and wonder where their energy and buoyancy came from, and why I had none. I'd remind myself of the tenets of mindfulness that I knew so well and then would fall into despair about how I was failing even that aspect of my life. What happened to everything I had learned about how to pause and open up space for whatever was arising? I couldn't even muster the energy for that.

My reset came when I enrolled in a mindfulness-based stress reduction program and remembered what it was like to hold my feelings with kindness. With my daily practice re-engaged, I could experience *both* the exhaustion and exhilaration of my life as a new parent. As I began attuning more to what I was feeling, I had an important insight that shifted things for me. Setting out on a walk one morning, I took a left-hand turn out of my driveway rather than turning right as I usually did. The right-hand turn was always my logical choice because there was a steep incline that I felt compelled to tackle up front. (And my brain was wired to "tackle" the hill rather than enjoy the walk.) But on this particular morning, I walked downhill. The gravity of the hill carried me, and I breathed a sigh of relief thinking, "This feels so good. I can just relax. I don't have to work so hard." This was such a simple recognition that it would have been easily missed had I not become aware of how depleted I was in those months of caregiving.

Walking downhill became part of my practice both literally and metaphorically. I began making sure that I allowed myself a "downhill slope" moment every day. I was learning to incline my mind toward ease despite the uphill challenges I often felt like I was facing. I incorporated gratitude into this practice, regularly naming the good things that I was feeling and experiencing, which was indispensable for further redirecting my mind in a positive way.

Until relatively recently, the dominant scientific view was that our brains were incapable of changing after we reached adulthood. But research in neuroscience has allowed us to see instead that our brains are remarkably malleable. We now know that we have the ability to forge new neural pathways, regardless of age, if we practice what we want to install. Rather than allowing our negativity, fear and pessimism to direct our actions, we can bring awareness to these habits of mind and pave a more positive path in our brains.

While we can't "think our way" to happiness, as positive thinking advocates want to have us believe, we can *practice* our way toward more positive states. We do this through meditation and mindfulness practice and by strengthening our inner resources like gratitude, compassion and positive emotions. In doing so, we can change the neuronal structure of our brains for the good. So, it is worth exploring: What influence do we want our minds to have on our brains, our lives and the world? How can mindfulness help us change our minds and our brains for the better?

Our Brain Default

Many of us can count on one hand the number of days each year in which we are fully embodying Psychologist Rick Hanson's (2009) "Five Cs" by being conscious, calm, contented, caring and creative. For me, these are the rare days in which everything falls into place—time feels abundant, the weather is pleasant and I am free of burdens. We all know what it feels like when we are truly centered, present and at ease, when our minds are quiet, hearts are open and we are living in "flow." But we don't often live from this place. Perhaps we can touch into the calm, contented, caring plane for a short period of time. But something pulls our attention away and we set off on a different path. Often that something is our monkey mind: our worries, distractions, an underlying sense of anxiety that something needs to get done, fixed or managed. Our default mode may be inhabiting a different set of Cs; Chaotic, Chronically stressed and Critical of ourselves.

Why is it that our activated brain tends to be the default? Why do we live most of our days from the perspective of what could go wrong rather than what might go right? The answer is that humans have evolved with a strong negativity bias. Our brains developed around very intense survival instincts. Remembering to enjoy a sunset didn't help us get out of harm's way when a predator was coming; our instincts to flee were far more protective. The habits that have been hardwired into our brains can get in the way of our ability to be present and positive. Yet research in neuroscience helps us understand that we can change the direction of the grooves in our brains, regardless of age or the extent of our habituated behavior. With commitment and intention, we can mindfully rewire our brains toward greater calm, contentment and compassion. But first, we have to understand why our brains get stuck in the default modes of activation and negativity.

Our Activated Brains

When we feel worried, overwhelmed or upset, our brains go into overdrive. When our brains are activated, our focus narrows and our bodies tense up. Some of us speed up when we get activated and we might talk, walk and work faster and harder. When I get overwhelmed, my control instinct kicks into high gear and I get intense about doing things, fixing things and checking things off my to-do list. Brendon often takes the opposite path—he slows down when he gets activated. One recent morning, we were both dealing with a stressful situation and trying to make breakfast. As I was zooming around, thinking about tasks ten steps ahead of what we were doing, I asked him why he was parked in the middle of the kitchen. He turned to me and said, "What, you don't like my inefficient way of making breakfast?" As annoyed as I was, I had to laugh at his sincerity.

Some people go into control overdrive when they are overwhelmed. Other people have an impulse to curl up in bed and shut the world out. Both sets of reactions are normal. The first reaction results from our "fight-or-flight" inheritance; our sympathetic nervous system's hardwired instinct to fight off the predator or get out of harm's way. The latter behavior results from the "freeze" instinct left over from our ancient reptilian brain that instructs our body to play dead so we won't get eaten by the predator. Both reactions can be wise, adaptive and helpful when we are actually in danger.

But the problem is that in our current day world of constant stress, our reactions aren't always in line with the nature or extent of the threat. Our worry about the future may be based on something we've created in our head rather than an imminent threat. And yet we often "lock" into these fight-flight-freeze reactions as our default, sometimes over long periods of time. In this case, our primitive emotional brains are running the show and we can't access the Five Cs.

There is an additional layer of reactivity that is worth mentioning here—our judging mind. When we get activated, the judging mind gets turned on: What's wrong with me? Why can't I handle this? These judgments might take the form of stories we replay in our heads like, "I'm a mess... a victim... a failure." We might anticipate that things will fall apart on account of our deficiencies. Or we might turn the judgments on others, in the form of blame: "You are the reason this project/ family/friendship is failing! You can't follow through!" We might blame everybody around us for all of the things that we perceive are going wrong. Our judging minds churn out false, inaccurate and destructive thoughts. These deceptive brain messages can create anger, anxiety and mistrust.

Early in my parenting journey, I did my share of blaming Brendon for falling short as a parent. I was angry that he was not the one to get up multiple times a night to breastfeed Aidan. I was frustrated that I was the one taking time out of my workday to go to Aidan's daycare center to nurse him during lunch. I didn't understand that his relationship with Aidan was developing around different needs and opportunities. I also didn't recognize that he didn't get to the enjoy 3:00 a.m. moments in which Aidan's soft body would relax into sleep in my arms. I was too angry about the injustices of human anatomy to care. These destructive thoughts were directed at him, but they were most detrimental to me. As the saying goes, "Holding onto anger is like drinking poison and expecting the other person to die."

Our reactivity comes from a deep place, and different people express it in different ways. Anger, anxiety and worry are all signals that we may need to look inward as we might be feeling powerless, hopeless or threatened. Reacting to our emotions may help us feel like we are taking control through some form of action, since our discomfort often comes from a place of feeling stuck or immobilized. So we go into "fix it" mode and add layers of negative thoughts and judgments onto our already activated brains, fueling the fires within. This moves us farther away from being able to access our caring, compassionate, contented self that is at the core of who we are.

While we can't expect contentment and ease all of the time, and we can't "will" ourselves happy, we can train our brains to incline our minds toward the Five Cs. In order to do so, we have to become aware of the habitual patterns that come from our negativity bias in order to loosen our identification with the stories and judgments that keep us locked into our activation cycle.

Our Negativity Bias

Rick Hanson (2016) suggests that our brains are like Velcro for negative experiences and Teflon for positive ones. The negative experiences stick to us. We remember them and they leave imprints in our brains. Conversely, positive experiences bounce off of us like Teflon. They are harder to recall and more difficult to generate since they haven't "protected" us in the same way that our negative experiences have. It makes sense that when we're down and out, the momentum of our negativity and pessimism can feel strong. Influencing the mind toward positivity, trying to tilt the scale, can feel like an uphill battle.

As I was trying to figure out how to manage the complicated transition as a parent, I stumbled on some important wisdom that gave me footing. My therapist handed me the book *Radical Acceptance* by Tara Brach who suggests that rather than fighting with the way that things are or trying to wrestle control out of an uncontrollable situation, we can bring curiosity and friendliness to what is happening. When I began bringing curiosity into my situation, rather than fear, I discovered that there might be a way to change my relationship with what was happening. Perhaps I could redirect my fear of failing and sense of overwhelm.

I had an insight one day that I could track, and make visible, the good things that were happening in my days. I bought a large poster board and I hung it up in the middle of the living room. I decided that it would be helpful to make visible my joys rather than continuing to shout out my frustration. In bright colors, I began to decorate this poster with each of the good things that I recalled from the day. I created what looked like a step ladder on the poster board. Starting on the lower left-hand corner, I listed the joys and each new day's additions were highlighted in the next rung of the ladder so that there was visible upward movement. This was the momentum I needed to see in order to feel like I was moving out of the stuck place.

Something happened as I tracked my daily positive moments and experiences. I watched as the step ladder rose higher and higher on my poster. In fact, I had to purchase additional posters and place them at higher spots on the wall to keep the upward momentum visible. I shared with Brendon details about what I wrote on the poster, naming the things that might otherwise have been hidden from view. Little by little, I could begin to see the light shining brighter in my life. I needed to see evidence of change on a daily basis, and this was the way I instinctively knew to do it.

Looking back now, I can see how this was a critical step in rewiring my brain away from the very strong energy of negativity and anxiety that had set in as I felt more and more overwhelmed. The fear was still there battling for my attention but there was something else directing my mind. Over time, I began to notice the good things as they were happening, rather than only when I had pen in hand and was searching for what to write. Gratitude became more accessible to me, and I could more easily appreciate the moments of joy as they arose.

We can shine light on our positive experiences in a way that has a powerful impact on our brains. Inclining the mind toward the positive can help to tip the imbalance of our negativity bias. This is called "positive neuroplasticity." It is not easy, and it can feel like swimming against the current when we are depressed, anxious and overwhelmed. Our brains get comfortable with the negativity bias and operating from fear. That familiarity is deeply rooted in the way our brain evolved, which explains why change is so difficult.

The Roots of Reactivity

The enduring nature of our negativity bias is easy to understand when we see how our brains evolved. While the "three brains" concept that I describe is a simplified version of our brain's evolution, it contextualizes the deep, primal roots of our reactivity. Our reptilian complex, the seed of our instincts, was the first part of the brain to develop. Our "survival brain" allows us to feel hunger, to know when to protect ourselves and to get out of dangerous situations. Our reptilian brain is still intact today in our human brain, and it is still responsible for our urges and instincts.

We later evolved our mammalian brain; the part of the brain that is the seat of our emotions. This is our limbic system which houses both our hippocampus and our amygdala. The hippocampus is associated with memory and the amygdala is the part of the brain that sends out alert signals to trigger our fight-or-flight reaction. As our "feeling brain" developed, we became able to identify what feels good and what doesn't feel good — and to remember that.

Most recently, we evolved our thinking brain, the "cortex" on the outside of the brain. This development allows us to reason and be thoughtful. We still have our survival instincts and we feel emotions; however, we can now try to reason our way through them. Our brains are far more complex than any other species on earth.

Despite our evolved brains which separate us from other species, we still react from our reptilian ("freeze") and limbic ("fight-or-flight") instincts. These instincts protect us without having to reason. But our brains sometimes don't know the difference between an immediate, life-threatening situation and a stressor like a work deadline, financial worry, relationship trouble or the overwhelm of parenting. With constant stress, the "on button" to our fight-or-flight reaction can get stuck. Our hormonal system which produces cortisol and adrenaline may go into overdrive for extended periods, even when the threat is over. The vigilance we used to maintain for the threat of a predator outside of us has now become internal.

Unlike the early days when our bodies down-regulated appropriately once we returned to safety after a tiger chase, our body-minds have a hard time returning to baseline when the on-button is jammed. We may stay stuck in our adrenalized state for quite a while. The looping cycle of fear, worry and anxiety can perpetuate this state. And this is where mindfulness comes in.

Taking the Seat of the Witness

Through mindfulness training and practice, we can change how our brain functions. Research shows that after eight weeks of practice we can decrease the brain cell volume of our amygdala and positively impact our fear response. The prefrontal cortex, which holds our memory of safety and is associated with awareness, concentration and decision making, can thicken on account of ongoing practice (Taren et al., 2013).[6]

How do we do this? As we learned in Chapter 2, we begin by pausing. Only then can we *notice* what is happening within us. With focused attention we can bring awareness to the contents of our minds, the sensations in our bodies and our feeling states and emotions. We can notice the reactivity, negativity, judgments and anxiety. We can bring objectivity to our thoughts or emotions by gently *labeling* them: worry, judgment, anxiety. Labeling emotions can calm the brain's emotional centers, including the amygdala. Bringing greater objectivity to our emotional experience can allow our reasoning and thinking center to come back online.

With this objectivity, we are "taking the seat of the witness," and becoming aware of the knowing itself. Only when we begin to see what is showing up in our minds and bodies can we skillfully work with what is arising rather than reacting to them. This requires that we don't reject what feels uncomfortable. It may not be wise to fully dive into the anxiety or fear but we might instead explore the edges of these states, examining what they feel or look like. We can get familiar with the discomfort. And if we sense resistance, we can get familiar with the resistance.

Mindfulness can shine the light of awareness on whatever it is that is bringing us discomfort. We can come to know what needs to happen next. Our rational mind may have ideas. But there is a deeper place of knowing and insight that can become available to us. As we raise our line of awareness, we are less likely to get hijacked by our fear and negativity bias, and more able to access our internal wisdom.

Thoughts Influence Behavior

There is no question that negative emotional states are sticky, and it is easy to get hijacked by our emotions. Hearing upsetting news or having a disagreement with a parent, child or boss might open up the floodgates of our negative emotions. A memory, fear or worry about something might trigger us. When we get upset, it often feels like the heightened emotional state will last forever. However, we know that each emotion we experience has a relatively short lifespan, an average of only about 1.5 minutes (Taylor, 2009).

Why does it feel like our heightened emotional states will last forever? Because our thoughts keep those emotions in circulation. If we're feeling sad, we might be thinking about the reasons we are feeling bad or telling ourselves stories that we will never be happy again. If we're angry we might find ourselves in blame mode, working out the details of how we were wronged or what we need to do to feel heard. We fuel our emotions with our thinking mind.

Problematically, the majority of our habitual thoughts tend to be negative. We marinate our minds with negativity. These thoughts leave tracks on our brains like a well-worn hiking trail. But we don't have to deepen the negative tracks. Just as negativity can get hardwired into our brains, the tracks of negativity can dissolve as we strengthen positive states. We know that neurons that fire together wire together. This is as true for when we fuel the fires of negativity as it is when we practice self-compassion and gratitude. If we continue to focus on negativity, the grooves of negativity grow deeper. If we focus on states like gratitude and compassion, we grow our capacity for positivity.

As my experience with the poster board shows, we can intentionally shift our attitude and orientation in a way that can bring us greater peace and ease. Our thoughts are only the beginning of change. In the words attributed to Gandhi: "Your beliefs become your thoughts, Your thoughts become your words, Your words become your actions, Your actions become your habits, Your habits become your values, Your values become your destiny." Our perceptual lens matters, and how we think can make an enormous, positive difference.

Installing Positivity

When my computer password expired during the difficult summer of 2020, I instinctively began creating a password similar to the other passwords I had used for the previous five years. Instead, I stopped myself and did something different. I thought about what password would most benefit my brain. The previous few months had been devastating between the ravages of the pandemic, the visceral pain of racial violence and the divisive politics in our country. So, I selected "HealthyWorld2020" as my new password. Cognizant of the many dimensions of sickness and suffering that our world was facing, I couldn't think of anything I wanted more. I didn't realize how powerful that password would be at the time. But I recalled and typed HealthyWorld2020 thousands of times before I was required to change my password the following year. Each time, I felt the positive energy behind that choice. I have since made it a daily practice of wishing for and imagining a Healthy World.

Research shows that we can't passively "will" ourselves to be happy. Positive thinking simply does not work that way. We have to make a concerted effort to rewire our brains through practice and repetition. We need to experience, on a somatic level, the inner states that we want to cultivate. My password experiment along with my good-things poster helped me see how important repetition is for changing my neuronal structure. As Rick Hanson (2016) argues, it is not only important to have positive thoughts, memories and experiences, but it is critical to "install" them into our brains and bodies. He suggests that we take the step of savoring and soaking our positive thoughts and experiences into our bodies. This might be recalling a good moment while lying in bed and imagining the experience getting absorbed into the body on a cellular level. Through repeating, enriching and absorbing our experiences, we can transform them from positive momentary states to beneficial lasting traits.

Hanson offers a practice called, "Taking in the Good" which involves four steps outlined by the acronym HEAL. These steps include having a positive experience, enriching it by holding it in the mind and body, absorbing it on a somatic and cellular level, and linking a positive experience with a negative one to weaken the negative association and strengthen the positive. This process is powerful in large part because we hold the positive experience in our body. This can counteract the distressing memories or emotions that get stuck in our body. Research shows that trauma, both minor and major traumatic experiences, are held in our bodies. As the saying goes, "the issues are in our tissues." Just as trauma can live in our bodies, so too can positive experiences inhabit our cells and tissues, counterbalancing the negative memories that occupy our bodies.

The Power of Gratitude

Gratitude is a magnifying glass when it comes to enhancing positive emotions. There is no shortage of research that emphasizes the positive benefits of gratitude. We know that it can strengthen the immune system, help us recover from loss and trauma, allow us to see the big picture and connect us with each other (Hanson, 2020). Gratitude positively impacts our health, our outlook on life and our wellbeing. And gratitude increases our experience of joy. We need to be present in the moment to experience gratitude. Conversely, the intentional practice of gratitude can help us stay present.

When we think about the experiences in our lives that were most enlivening, gratifying or meaningful, the common denominator is that we were in our bodies to experience them and to register what was happening. This might include experiencing a birth or death, a moment of giving, authentic connection or simple appreciation. We feel an aliveness in our hearts when we experience gratitude. Being present in our bodies allows us to directly access our experiences. Our mindfulness practice can direct us back to our bodies, to the present moment, where gratitude can be directly experienced.

There are simple things we can do to plant seeds of gratitude, to make it more present in our lives and to soak it in and savor it. Some examples might include:

- Beginning the day with a thought or prayer of gratitude. This might include appreciation for your warm bed, a new day, a chance to do things better.
- Throughout the day stopping and noticing the mug of warm tea in your hands, the cat purring on your lap, the sunshine on your face. Set a timer as a reminder to practice gratitude throughout the day.
- Keeping a journal of three good things that you record at the end of every day. Let those experiences soak into your heart and your body as you drift off to sleep.
- Sharing gratitude outwardly by directly communicating your appreciation or writing a "gratitude letter" to someone who you have not previously thanked.
- Smiling as you go about your day. Smile to your neighbor, your co-worker, the grocery store clerk. And say, with sincerity: "Thank you. I really appreciate it" or "I really appreciate you."

When you begin practicing gratitude, you might notice that you have to intentionally look for good things. But as you continue, you'll find that your awareness changes. You may start noticing good things more frequently. You don't have to look for them after a while. Rather than coming home at the end of the day listing off problems, you might find yourself sharing pleasant and positive things that happened. When we get into the habit of this practice, our perspective changes. We see positive things that we didn't see before.

There are so many ways that gratitude and seeding positivity can help us. Research shows that it can lower our stress response, increase our psychological resilience, lift our mood and protect against depression (Hanson, 2007). When we are more positive, we are more motivated to do things that are beneficial for ourselves and others. Practicing positivity can also help us let go of the mental narratives that fuel our negativity bias. The more we practice positivity, the more our brain synapses strengthen toward positivity. As we cultivate mindful awareness and seed positivity, we can experience more direct contact with life. Not only are we more conscious of everything within and around us, but we can remove the barriers that prevent us from being the calm, contented, caring and creative people that we know ourselves to be. We can more easily access our authentic core, who we really are.

The Power of Choice

When we believe our negative thoughts and stories and allow our activated brains to direct our behaviors, we can easily find ourselves putting negativity into the world. A different option is available when we bring awareness to our thoughts and stories; we have a choice of how we want to respond to and engage with the world. While our choices lie on an individual level, our thoughts and actions impact the collective. No behavior is inconsequential. The classic story of "The Two Wolves," that went viral on the Internet after September 11, beautifully illustrates this point:

One evening an old Cherokee told his grandson about a battle that goes on inside people.

He said, "My son, the battle is between two wolves inside us all. One is Evil—It is anger, envy, jealousy, sorrow, regret, greed, arrogance, self-pity, guilt, resentment, inferiority, lies, false pride, superiority, and ego.

"The other is Good—It is joy, peace, love, hope, serenity, humility, kindness, benevolence, empathy, generosity, truth, compassion and faith."

The grandson thought about it for a minute and then asked his grandfather: "Which wolf wins?"

The old Cherokee simply replied, "The one you feed."

The skills we develop to counteract our negativity bias and to install positive emotions, gratitude and appreciation are critical not just on an individual level. These are the skills that we need to help build a just, caring and compassionate world. While mindfulness is a personal practice—no one can do it for us—the ripples of our practice extend infinitely outward. As Kabat-Zinn suggests, "When our doing comes out of being, out of awareness, it is likely to be a wiser, freer, more imaginative, more creative, and more caring doing, a doing that can itself catalyze greater wisdom, compassion and healing in the world and in your own heart" (2019, p. 14). As we will see in the next chapter, those ripples of wisdom and compassion can be powerful mediators for the waves that ceaselessly crash around us and our world. The direction in which we choose to aim our minds, during both the calm and stormy moments, can make all the difference.

***

Practice: Noticing Thoughts

Find a comfortable seated position. Take a few deep breaths as you settle in. Then allow your breath to follow its natural rhythm and rest your attention on your breath, wherever it is most natural for you. That might be noticing the air coming in and out of your nose or the rising and falling of your chest or belly. Establish a steady attention on your breath for a few moments, letting yourself come into presence.

You will notice, after not too long, that your mind has begun to wander. When you notice that thoughts are arising, see if you can bring a kind attention to the thoughts or the planning, stories or images that are coming up. You might name them gently, using terms like "thinking," "planning," "doubt" or "fear." As you name them, let the thoughts show themselves to you so you can know them. As you give space to your thoughts by noticing and naming them, you might find that they begin to soften and dissipate. When they do, and they're no longer calling your attention, you can return to your breath.

This is a gentle, simple practice that acknowledges, but doesn't judge, the busy mind. The intent is not to change or dismiss your thoughts but to simply get to know the contents of your mind. As you practice, you might notice how long your thoughts really stay around. Do you find that some thoughts move through your mind instantaneously while others are more "sticky"? What happens when you turn your attention *toward* your thoughts? You might ask yourself some additional questions as you strengthen your awareness of thoughts: What stories do I repeatedly tell myself? What is my busy mind preventing me from feeling? What are my thoughts trying to protect me from? Getting to know the contents of your mind takes focus but it can be a deeply informative practice.

Chapter 5

Turning toward Emotional Difficulty

When we do the work, the wounds become wisdom.
—Daniel Baylis

We all know what it's like to get tossed around by emotional waves. It's not comfortable. In fact, it can be excruciating. So, we often choose to distract ourselves, avoid our feelings and hide out in whatever brings us the most comfort in the moment. The powerful waves of our emotions can push against our efforts at mindfulness, making it difficult to welcome or get curious about what is happening. Yet, by staying open in the moments of difficulty, we can learn to ride the waves of our emotions rather than getting tossed around by them. Our practice can lead us toward the calm, still pool of water that exists beneath the waves. While we may not always be able to access it, we can learn to trust that it is there.

The waves that I encounter have not become less frequent on account of my mindfulness practice. They keep coming, and intensifying, at their will. But my trust has become deeper over the years in my capacity to handle whatever is happening. I have learned that I can relax into the emotional waves rather than fighting them fruitlessly. Meditating for periods of time on retreat has helped to give me confidence that not only can I withstand the discomfort of the waves, but I can find stillness in which to rest, despite the turbulence. These experiences have impacted my daily life and given me the courage to persevere, and trust myself, even in the midst of my most challenging moments.

My ability to find shelter in the storm came as a surprise to me two days into a week-long silent retreat. My sleep had been disturbed the night before by chaotic dreams that left me deeply unsettled. I dreamt of co-workers who wouldn't leave my house and family members who needed me to sort through a mound of their personal items before I could get to an urgent appointment. I woke up at 5:00 a.m. wondering why these dreams came to visit me.

On my cushion that morning, the chaos came back in the form of what had been left undone and was waiting for me at home. "Really?" I thought. "I'm on retreat. Can't I just have some peace?" Of course, I knew that was the wrong question. So, I took a breath and held out a welcome mat to the feelings. I let the anxiety wash over me and felt the tension in my body. It got pretty intense, and I wondered if I would get sucked into its vortex. So, I asked myself a question: "How can I be with the energy in this moment?" What came to me was an image of myself sitting calmly in the middle of a swirling, tornadic field of energy. I breathed into that space of calm and serenity. And then I asked myself, "What can support me in this space?" Aidan and Brendon came to mind, and I saw us like three Buddha nesting dolls. I felt Aidan's calm body in front of me and Brendon's serenity behind me. The swirling energy continued around us. But we had a solid, stable, calm space to rest together. The vortex eventually lifted, and I continued to experience the safety of my nestled family.

Even in the quietest moments, the things we repress, ignore, reject and struggle with have a way of making themselves known. And then we have a choice: How do we want to be with the waves? We could banish them or approach them with anger or disgust. But another option is to relax and let go into the discomfort. I've spent hours, days at a time, getting caught up in the energy of my emotional waves. But I've learned that there are places to rest within the waves when I can remember to relax. I've also learned that storms don't last forever. The energy will shift and change when I stop trying so hard to control things.

Mindfulness contains infinite wisdom for helping us learn how to let go. When we stop fighting or rejecting our emotions and open space for them instead, we can find that there is a lot to learn from how we navigate the waves and winds of our lives. This practice can become a gateway to greater awareness and self-compassion.

Learning to Stay

Despite taking him to obedience school, Brendon and I failed miserably at training our dog, Chipper. We didn't put the effort into the follow up, so Chipper continued to jump on us, bark at strangers and beg for table scraps. We had watched dozens of *Dog Whisperer* segments over the years, and we understood that for a dog to learn to stay, it must overcome its instinctual behaviors, habitual patterns and deeply rooted desires. This requires training, diligence and human commitment. These were investments we hadn't made until our neighbor hinted at how annoyed they were getting with Chipper's barking.

Like our pet friends, humans, too, find it difficult to resist their instinctual tendencies. We don't often recognize how easily we allow ourselves to get carried away by the energy of our emotions. We may indulge our hurt by marinating in stories of victimhood or stoke our fear by catastrophizing worst-case-scenarios. We often infuse our stories with blame and shame and turn on ourselves or others when we are emotionally activated. And rather than exploring what is happening, we tend to look away and run as fast as we can when we feel the pangs of discomfort.

We push uncomfortable or strong emotions away so we don't have to feel what might be nagging at us. But pushing away our emotions and turning away from what we're feeling can be exhausting. It's like knowing that there is a child within us who needs to be tended to. But we don't want to take the time or put the energy towards this child's needs. The needs don't go away nor does the nagging feeling. But we expend a lot of energy pretending they will.

Rather than calming and soothing our anxious minds, pushing difficult emotions away can have the opposite effect. We know well that what we resist persists. In not attending to what is asking for attention, the rejected emotion only gets more intense. And when we get involved in our stories of blame, shame and judgment, we further divert ourselves from experiencing the truth of what we are feeling. When we listen to the messages that our emotions are trying to tell us, we can hear their intelligence. The Greeks referred to anger as a "noble emotion" because they understood that anger had a purpose. In Latin American culture, "nervios" is considered to be a physical condition marked by certain characteristics like emotional upset, trembling and heat in the body. It is common for someone struggling with acute stress to give it the name "nervios" which acknowledges the condition. In these cases, the experience of upset and difficult emotions are named rather than rejected or denied. This stands in contrast to how Americans are culturally taught to suppress, hide and contain our emotions.

We rarely examine the cost of suppressing behaviors when it comes to difficult emotions. Besides the exhaustion of ignoring the needs that our deeper self knows are there, we tend to indulge in unhealthy escape habits. We might turn to comfort eating, drinking or substances. We might obsessively worry, stoke our anxiety or catastrophize rather than touching into the fear or grief that are at the root of these behaviors. Or we might lock into judgment—focusing on what's wrong with the other person or with ourselves—pushing our own truths or those of others away rather than looking honestly at the situation. We can spend our entire lives playing the blame and shame game. Sometimes we think that is an easier game to play than getting real with ourselves. But we know, down deep inside, it's not.

We often assume that we can control which emotions we want to experience. But as Brené Brown (2010) points out, "We cannot selectively numb emotions, when we numb the painful emotions, we also numb the positive emotions." The "easy" strategy of avoidance and numbing can backfire, for when we cut ourselves off from our heart, we can't access our wisdom. We can't really grow. And that is where many of us get stuck. There is a cost to our emotional dissociation.

Learning to stay can be a profoundly challenging process. Like a dog in training, it requires diligence and commitment. Unlike the kick in the pants that our neighbors' annoyance with Chipper caused, we are typically not motivated by someone telling us that our behaviors are destructive. We have to find our intrinsic motivation to lean in when things get difficult. This motivation often comes only when nothing else has worked. But we can cultivate it intentionally by bringing mindful awareness to the habitual tendencies that keep us locked in a place of resistance and avoidance. Unfortunately, our culture teaches the opposite—distract, avoid, repeat. Perhaps only when we're aware that we are not finding relief from "business as usual" are we ready to commit to doing things differently. Only then can acceptance, rather than avoidance, become a logical choice.

Making Space

Making space for our emotional waves is an important part of our practice. This can be a challenge when emotions run high. A few years ago, I had an explosive fallout with some colleagues at work. A difficult meeting ended with harsh words that stung me deeply. I was spinning in my anger, indulging my feelings of victimhood and charting my course to set these people straight. For three days I had to calm my impulse to write that angry email. I closely observed my anger over those days. I would mentally note where I was: 80% angry, 50% angry, 30% angry, and so on. As my anger began to subside, I started to see things more clearly. I saw how I contributed to the misunderstanding, how I made choices that did not uphold the spirit of our agreement, how I didn't communicate wisely. My role in the conflict became clear in a way that wasn't available to me immediately after the argument.

When one of my colleagues reached out, half blaming but half reconciling, I was able to latch onto the reconciliation portion of her note. Instead of blaming back, I saw where there was an opening for beginning again with respectful communication. I let her know that I wanted to try doing our communication better. I couldn't have responded in this way the first few days after the fallout. But after noticing, naming and giving space to my emotions, my rational, caring brain was able to come back online. This was in no way a linear process. I jumped from rational mind to emotional mind and back again over those three days until I started seeing more clearly. I made sure to observe which part of the brain was steering the wheel. And I allowed myself to be angry and gave myself some grace.

Mindfulness does not offer an immediate solution for our emotional pain. We can't just "become mindful" and act with civility and equanimity when our limbic system has been hijacked. Even after a lifetime of meditation practice, our self-defeating habitual behaviors will come back again and again. As the late Ram Dass (2014) described, after decades of practice, his neuroses were alive and well. The difference, he explained, was that he was eventually able to experience them as "friendly little Shmoos."

One benefit I have noticed to come from my mindfulness practice has been that the lag time has decreased between when I get triggered and when I can respond thoughtfully. I call this my "kitchen awareness" since I tend to have my most volatile reactions to triggers in the kitchen. Now, rather than flying off of the handle and staying activated for long periods of time, I am much quicker to recognize when I am triggered and to bring kind awareness to the moment. This doesn't mean that I never fly off the handle or that I don't ever react with anger or aggression. But it does mean that I can see much more clearly what is happening, even when I chose to indulge my emotions and step into the battle. "Clear seeing" allows us to catch true glimpses of cause and reaction and our role in everything that happens.

Surrendering Control

With practice, we can learn to give our emotions space in the heat of the moment. We can also learn how to slow down the reactivity chain. But what about working with emotions like fear and anxiety that are long-standing and deeply ingrained within us? It is inevitable that we will experience fear that festers over long periods of time before our awareness catches up to it.

Fear can be an underlying energy behind so many emotions and experiences—anxiety, anger, sadness, rage. Most of the time, we are not aware that fear lies beneath the surface of our emotions. Our anticipation of helplessness, along with accumulated experiences from our childhood and our personal history of trauma, may keep us in a contracted stance of fear. Rather than reacting to the threat of triggers outside of us we may get reactive from within. When we can see more clearly through the cobwebs of our minds, we can begin to unpack fear's complex tangle. It is worth examining this root emotion and how it naturally gets disguised, banished and amplified in our plight for comfort and security. As mindfulness teaches us, when we open up to fear rather than retracting and when we move our fear out of the shadows, we can decrease its power over us.

I had been practicing mindfulness for many years before I really came to know the emotion of fear. I realized later that fear had been with me all along. I just got really good at keeping it at bay. But when it came up for me with full intensity after

Aidan was born, it became a force to recon with. I literally couldn't move forward in my life until I stepped into my fear and learned what it was all about. I had tried bypassing it for years. And it manifested in anxiety. I didn't recognize that to work with anxiety, I'd have to get to know my fear.

Insomnia was the symptom that forced me to confront all of this. After running myself ragged in my new role as a mom, my nervous system became overloaded and forced me to stop. Aidan was a terrible sleeper for his first eight months. When he started sleeping through the night, I stopped. It didn't help that our 18-year-old dog, in her last phase of life, had taken to nocturnal digging in our closet. But I'm not really sure that any of that mattered. As so many people who have experienced chronic insomnia know, once the pattern has set in of wakefulness, anxiety (How long is this going to continue?), more wakefulness, more anxiety (How am I going to function tomorrow?), repeated night after night, it is difficult to stop the train wreck.

My waking life became more and more focused on the "problem" and my anxiety went through the roof. My turn-around began when I found a therapist who did not tell me I could fix the problem. Instead, she set me on a path toward accepting where I was, and she helped me learn to work with— rather than against—what was happening. Only then could I notice the layers of fear that were blocking my way from any kind of resolution. I encountered my controlling self and its fear of letting go, into this new life and the new dependencies, along with fears about what could happen if I couldn't hold it together. There were fears of failing my son, not being able to manage my work and letting down my husband. Then there were the fears of not being lovable since I felt I was such a terrible mess. Deeper still were the fears of mentally breaking from stress and lack of sleep: Will this ever change? What will I have to give up? Who will I become if I never recover?

There was one night when the fear had become particularly unbearable. I sought out a meditation practice on fear and my Google search led me to a video talk by Pema Chödrön. As I listened to her speak, I fell into a deep sleep. There was something powerful about her acknowledgment of the universal experience of fear and her message that we never have stood on solid ground to begin with. It reminded me of a discussion, many years prior, that my meditation group had after reading Pema Chödrön's book *When Things Fall Apart*. We dove into the metaphor of life being like floating on a raft in the middle of a body of water with no oars. Back then, I was horrified about the concept of having no oars. No control? Free floating in a dangerous, vast body of water with no paddle? And here I was being asked—forced—to accept this truth of groundlessness in my own life. I had no oars!

That difficult night, the truth fully sunk in. Rather than pushing the fear away, I finally surrendered into it. I knew with complete certainty that there was no escaping. I either had to let go into the fear or I would continue a fruitless battle that would leave me feeling helpless. That was a major turning point for me. It by no means resolved my insomnia or the day-to-day struggles but it confirmed with absolute certainty what I had to do. I had to get curious about this fear and befriend it in order to learn what it had to teach me. In many ways, I look at my life as "before insomnia" and "after insomnia" given how much I have grown as a result of learning how to lean into and let go of my fear. And I'm still learning, I'll always be learning. As Tara Brach suggests, "Facing fear is a lifelong training in letting go of all we cling to" (2004, p. 193).

My ability to open up space for the fear and to surrender control could only happen because I was willing to stay with the discomfort. As Pema Chödrön describes:

"Things falling apart is a kind of testing and also a kind of healing. We think that the point is to pass the test or to overcome the problem, but the truth is that things don't really get solved. They come together and they fall apart... The healing comes from letting there be room for all of this to happen" (1997, p. 8).

Fear can bring about our most intense internal judgments. It aggravates the "trance of unworthiness" that we all experience to some extent. And it can force us to experience vulnerability in a profoundly uncomfortable way. I had to learn to talk about my struggles, to embrace my imperfections and to trust that others wouldn't abandon me. My mindfulness practice held me steady enough to do this work. It reminded me to drop the judgments and offered a supportive, loving basin for my vulnerability.

We are hardwired to turn away from what we fear; this is how our bodies and minds evolved to respond to threats. We work against our evolutionary engineering when we turn to face our demons. Yet, if we can tap into our courage and turn towards what we are afraid of, we might see the demons for what they are: fleeting experiences, beliefs and stories. Those beliefs and stories can feel real and intense. They might constitute well-worn grooves in our brains or reflect conditioning from a previous trauma. But if we can bring them into the light, we might find that our emotional demons can no longer hold us hostage. And, as Brené Brown (2010) suggests, we might discover that, "The dark does not destroy the light; it defines it. It's our fear of the dark that casts our joy into the shadows."

I still have sleepless nights. But I no longer believe that I have a "problem." The problem vanished when my fear abated. The space which that fear used to occupy is now covered with the fertile soil of compassion. I know how to care for myself when I have sleep difficulties and I share a deep connection with all people who struggle in this particular way.

Stepping Out of Fear

Fear often lives below the line of consciousness, and we may only recognize it when the alarm bell of the amygdala gets jammed, as my experience of insomnia illustrates. When we push against our emotions, they will inevitably push back harder. Jon Kabat-Zinn's work with pain patients at the Stress Reduction Clinic at the University of Massachusetts Medical Center highlights how pushing against physical pain locks patients into a cycle of suffering. He focused his work on helping his patients learn to relate *to* the pain rather than react *from* it. As has been well documented, mindfulness-based stress reduction has been found to positively impact the experience of pain. The program doesn't purport to eliminate pain but rather free patients from some degree of suffering (Kabat-Zinn, 1990).

Both physical and emotional pain can trigger a cycle of suffering. Psychiatrist Daniel Siegel (2009) describes our reactivity chain using the example of back pain. The experience of back pain initiates a trigger to worry, which instigates a set of beliefs about what's going to happen. Worried thoughts activate anxiety which can cause the muscles to further tense and tighten. Tight muscles increase the pain, which can trigger more worried thoughts. These thoughts cause us to tense up more. We look for relief and try to push away the pain. When these strategies don't work, we are re-triggered, and the cycle begins again.

As I described in Chapter 3, we begin throwing second arrows once we are triggered by the experience of pain. If we can bring mindful awareness to what is happening early on, once we feel the initial trigger of pain, we have a choice to limit the arrows that we throw. When we choose to bring awareness to what is happening — rather than ignoring or controlling it — we may find that we can tolerate the pain enough to notice our resistance to it and maybe even to explore it a bit. If we can do this with kindness, we may sense that the pain is not as solid as it seemed, and we might notice that it changes and transforms. This awareness helps us recognize that we are not the pain. It allows us to gain some distance from the pain. As Psychologist

Shauna Shapiro described in her book *Good Morning, I Love You*, when her grandfather applied mindfulness to his suffering from the debilitating pain of osteoarthritis, he recognized that "The part of me that sees the pain is not the part of me that is in pain. My awareness of the pain is not in pain" (2020, p. 109). When his relationship to the pain shifted, he had the space to re-engage with his life. As this example shows, our awareness can reverse the cycle of suffering when we become an active observer of the changing nature of the pain rather than a victim of it.

Unpacking this cycle of pain shines a light on some key lessons that can we apply to working with emotional pain:

1. Our efforts to control and fix the "problem" can trap us into making things worse. Our ability to "be with" whatever is going on can help to loosen the trap.
2. Symptoms are like the weather; we can't necessarily influence how or when they arise, but we can influence how we relate to them. We can know what we can fruitfully control and when we can benefit from letting go of our efforts to control (Siegel, 2009).
3. The two arrows are distinct—emotional and physical pain are different from worry and fear. If the arrows can be uncoupled, and the second (and third) arrows dropped, then suffering can leave and only the experience of pain remains.

Kabat-Zinn (1990) suggests that suffering is only one response to pain. Another response is curiosity and acceptance. Instead of asking, "Why is this difficulty here?" or "Why doesn't it go away?" we can ask "How does difficulty work in my life? What is it trying to tell me?" The pain can become an object of exploration rather than a cause for fear. Wise discernment is important here. There are times when the wise choice is not to sit in the heat of emotional or physical distress or stay with the waves of fear or anxiety. We have to be aware of our window of tolerance and maintain neutral or safe places to rest in body and mind when we are in pain, activated, anxious or overwhelmed.

Wise Discernment

I learned about wise discernment when I was settling in for a morning of meditation while having frightening heart palpitations. It was the morning after I had arrived at a mountain cabin 8000 feet above sea level for a self-guided retreat. Earlier in the morning, I had taken a hearty walk up and down the surrounding hills. I then got on my yoga mat outside to stretch and as soon as I stood up, my heart started pounding furiously. It frightened me. I thought I knew what to do—observe what was happening, without judgment. Name what was arising. Bring compassion to my moment-to-moment experience. Keep breathing.

So, I sat with these disconcerting palpitations. I named them "heart beating." I put my hand on my heart, wishing my heart well. Anxiety arose. I named it "anxiety" anxiety. Then the flood of catastrophic thinking started. "Will I need to go to the nearest hospital? Is this retreat doomed?" So, I named all of that—"worry" worry. As the minutes wore on, my body and mind were in such upheaval that I instinctively kept jumping off of my cushion, wanting to run into the cabin, somehow toward safety. So, I named that—"fear" fear.

Ten minutes went on and the heart pounding was not changing or going away. My relationship with my situation was not shifting. I was moving through the same cycle of anxiety that Daniel Siegel describes in his back pain example. I went from worry, to stories, to anxiety, to tension and back to worry. And I realized that noticing the throbbing heartbeat and leaning into it was not going to help me. I thought about my options. If I gave up on meditating and went inside the cabin, I would probably continue to focus on the anxiety, just unskillfully. There was little inside to distract me.

So, I did something different. I stood up. I noticed my feet. I felt them firmly on the ground. I moved my attention out of my head and my chest and into my feet. And I recognized that the best course of action would not be to give up on meditating but to switch to a walking meditation practice. I found a good path to walk on, paid attention to the sensations in my feet and breathed deeply. As I began to settle into the walking, my mind became less fixated on the palpitations. I would occasionally check in with my heart. And I would name the throbbing and breathe deeply and place my attention back on my feet and their contact with the ground. In the course of 30 minutes, the palpations began to pass.

This distressful situation had a relatively quick resolution. Had it not, I would have done the appropriate thing and sought out medical care. But so many of our distressing situations naturally resolve themselves. We can support ourselves by what we choose to do in moments of distress. Our strategies for managing pain, difficulty and fear need to come from understanding our window of tolerance and how to stay steady in the moment. We need to care for ourselves with kindness and compassion. And when we allow ourselves to stay present with what is happening, we find that we know what to do.

Riding the Waves

There are steps that we can take on and off the cushion to help us skillfully ride the waves of emotion. We can apply this set of lessons in all areas of our lives.

Notice and Name What Is Happening

When we feel an emotional wave coming on, we can stop, pay attention and make contact with the immediate sensation of the emotion. We might simply ask ourselves: "What is happening right now?" When sadness is arising, we might notice what it feels like in our heart. If it is anxiety, we might notice discomfort in our belly. We might find that our shoulders have tightened, our heart may be pounding or a heaviness has set in. We can notice these sensations without judgment and allow them to be what they are. Both physical and psychological manifestations of emotional distress can be detected in the body when we shine the light of awareness on them.

Once we've noticed what is coming up, we can give it a gentle name—"There is sadness. There is anxiety." And then we breathe into the feeling of sadness or the heart space that is holding it. We might find ourselves telling a story about what we are feeling, and we can name that too—"victim story," "fear story," "not-good-enough story." We can train our mind to notice these patterns, stories and beliefs. Labeling allows emotions to move from the personal sphere—*I am* anxious, fearful or angry to an objective space—*here is* anxiety, fear or anger.

Daniel Siegel (2014) offers a strategy he calls "Name It to Tame It." He explains that the right hemisphere of our brain is the seat of our pain and strong emotions. The left hemisphere makes sense of what's going on in the right hemisphere. If our left brain can name what's happening—"anxiety" or "fear"—then the neurotransmitters in the right hemisphere are soothed. We can calm our brain simply by acknowledging what is happening.

Explore the Emotion with Kind Curiosity

Rather than using distractions or control strategies when we feel emotional intensity, we can explore it with some curiosity. We might ask ourselves: How big is this sadness? How deep is the grief? How intense is this anxiety? We can examine its shape, size and density. If it feels too big, we move our attention to a part of our body that feels neutral like our hands or our feet and then return to noticing the size and shape of the emotion when we are ready.

We aren't taught to face what is uncomfortable or difficult. But our practice of turning toward the difficulty can help us to disarm the emotion. There's a story about a child who has a recurring dream about getting chased by a bear. The child wakes up horrified every time she has this dream. Her wise grandmother suggests that instead of running from the bear, perhaps in the next dream she should try to turn and face it. Find out what it actually looks like, the grandma suggested. The next time the dream happens, the child turns to face the bear. To her astonishment, it's much smaller than she thought and not scary at all. She realizes that there is nothing to be afraid of. The bear dream never returned.

When it comes to our fears or difficult emotions, we might find the same thing—that there is far less to be afraid of than we initially thought. But it also may be the case that it is not safe to turn toward and face the bear of our fears. Instead, we might explore its edges. We can do that by turning toward, little by little, investigating, breathing into the fear and working around the edges. How big is this fear? Which part is sharp? What part can I make space for? How much can I be with this? When we accept our emotions rather than pushing them away, we might find that they intensify, begin to dissipate or shift in the body. As we watch the emotions change, we can recognize their impermanent nature.

Stabilize through Resourcing

Developing our inner resources, or resourcing, when we're not in distress is good preparation for the difficult times. We can identify images, beings or places that help us to relax and feel centered. We can bring these resources to mind to help us stabilize during turbulent times. For example, we might call to mind a loving being who represents wisdom and light and imagine their presence surrounding us or holding us. We can bring to mind a place that brings us comfort like a setting in nature that we love, a place from our past that made us feel safe or some other peaceful place like a lake or mountain. Yet, it is not enough to simply visualize these images. We need to activate and install our inner resources by experiencing them somatically, letting them absorb into our bodies. As Rick Hanson (2020) suggests, we want to directly experience what we want to grow so that it can become a mental habit. Imagining and feeling how these resources make us feel safe and steady can be part of our regular practice.

When we are resourced, we feel more centered and able to lean into our emotions. From this place, we can slowly expand our window of tolerance. We don't push our window of tolerance open, but we notice what we are capable of handling (perhaps with a little stretch) and we allow more in as our steadiness grows. Spending time in nature, walking or doing yoga might help to center and steady us. Talking to someone we trust, listening to music or doing art can also bring a sense of stability. With mindful awareness, we will know what is needed. We simply need to listen to ourselves.

Open to Compassion

When we are living with emotional distress, we tend to feel isolated because others can't see that we're suffering. Unlike a physical malady like a broken leg, our emotional pain lies hidden beneath the surface. Experiencing fear, anxiety and depression may make us more hesitant to reach out to others. When we feel bad, we can lock into feelings of shame and self-contempt which further increases our sense of separation from others.

If we allow ourselves to open to what is happening and to be vulnerable in its midst, we have the potential to decrease our experience of isolation. When we understand that, just like us, everyone suffers, our suffering becomes less personal. Our pain can become a gateway to compassion. If we can cultivate compassion for ourselves in our moments of suffering, this caring can be extended outward to others who are suffering.

With a receptive and accepting attitude, we can bear witness to our emotional suffering rather than being the suffering itself. When we observe our emotions with kindness, we might find that our difficulty can be held in a larger awareness that is loving and kind. As is illustrated in Kabat-Zinn's lake meditation, "We sit with the intention to hold in awareness and acceptance all the qualities of mind and body, just as the lake sits held, cradled, contained by the earth" (2005, p. 143). We can find that there is something larger than our small self that is holding us. And then we can let our difficulties wake up our heart of compassion.

Calm amidst the Storm

Practicing mindfulness can help us build confidence that we can safely be with the waves of our emotions and even find stillness amidst the storms in our lives. On many occasions, I have been surprised to find that there is a space in which to rest when I relax and stop resisting the waves. I have seen many others have this experience. One student I was recently working with was struggling with her cousin's cancer diagnosis and her son's substance addiction. She was baffled as to why she was anxious and intensely focused on her to-do list. When I led her through a somatic guided meditation, she identified a storm that was centered in her chest. She observed the storm's wrath, the winds and the rain. As she breathed in and out of the storm, she noticed that its intensity shifted and changed. And she recognized that she didn't want the storm to completely go away. So, we focused on what she needed to do to protect herself in the midst of the storm. She identified a purple rain jacket that was comforting and protective. And then she found peace walking in the storm, letting the wind and the rain come down on her purple rain jacket. She needed to be with the pain of the storm, and she found a way to be both present and safe in its midst.

Sylvia Boorstein (1996) points out, "Mindfulness meditation doesn't change life. Life remains as fragile and unpredictable as ever. Meditation changes the heart's capacity to accept life as it is." If we are willing to stay open, we can honor rather than reject the waves and storms of our lives. We don't have to be imprisoned by them or go to war with them, making them our enemy. They can be accepted for what they are: part of this shifting, changing experience of being human. As we will see in the next chapter, learning to stay open to the uncertainty in life, and surrendering to the experience of groundlessness, is a powerful practice that can allow us to experience freedom of heart and mind, even as the winds of change are blowing.

**

Practice: Making Space for Emotions

Begin this practice by taking a few deep full breaths to collect your attention. Then let your breath resume its natural rhythm and focus your attention on your breathing or the sensations in your hands or feet for a few minutes as you've done before.

When you feel present and anchored, let the breath recede into the background. Now place your attention on your heart space, noticing the state of your emotions, the primary object of focus for this practice. Take this moment and feel how your emotions manifest in your body— perhaps you can notice your heart rate or breathing rhythm. Maybe your attention is drawn to a feeling of sadness in your heart or tension in your shoulders. Perhaps your belly is the seat of your emotions, and you have the sensation of butterflies or anxiety.

Try to investigate these sensations with an attitude of interest or curiosity. You don't need to ask yourself why the sensations are arising or what they mean but you are just noticing how they feel in your body from moment to moment. Does anything shift as you sit with the sensations or emotions? Can you sit with them with kindness and tenderness? If a strong emotion comes up, you might choose to put your hand on your heart and make a physical connection with yourself, perhaps even breathing into your heart space. As you have done before, whenever your mind begins to wander away, gently bring it back to the breath or the heart space.

Notice if your impulse is to flee the emotion or sensation or to leave the practice altogether. That is perfectly normal. If that impulse arises, you might name it "resistance," "repulsion" or whatever is coming up for you. But the idea here is to stay with what is happening in the body for this moment and the next, rather than trying to make it go away.

Just like in our awareness of thoughts meditation, when you bring kind attention to a sensation or emotion, you might find that it dissipates or dissolves. While emotions and sensations may feel strong or solid at times, we begin to notice that they are like any other part of our experience: impermanent and perpetually changing.

Chapter 6

Surrendering to Groundlessness

In the choice to let go of your known way of being, the whole world is revealed to your new eyes.
—Danna Faulds

I am the first to go kicking and screaming into change. When I was in my 20s, I threw a fit when my roommate told me she was moving. I didn't like her. We were a bad match. And yet the idea of change and disruption got me unhitched. Twenty years later, when my boss announced her retirement, I seethed. While I knew it was her time to move on, I was annoyed that my work life would have to change, and I would be forced to adapt to a new way of doing things.

We all have to face change at one point or another. Moderate change can be disruptive, at best. When change is sudden and significant, it can shatter our sense of stability. Naturally, we become reactive and resistant in times of change. We might get angry or fearful or deny what is happening when the change feels like it is more than we can handle. But when we are forced to face change head on, we have no choice but to confront the immovable truth of groundlessness. If we are willing to see it, we find that clinging to the way that we want things to be only leads to additional suffering.

There are few experiences of groundlessness more intense than facing a health scare. While dreadful to go through, these moments force us to call upon the inner resources that we often forget we have available to us. I was recently called for further testing after a suspicious mammogram. In the week that I spent waiting for the appointment, I lost all sense of rationality as

I became convinced that a cancer diagnosis was imminent. I began believing my story about the worst-case scenario.

While I was waiting to be called to the X-ray room, I scanned my phone and discovered an unopened email with a quote of the day. With surprise, I read Pema Chödrön's words from her book *When Things Fall Apart*: "When we cling to thought and memories, we are clinging to what cannot be grasped. When we touch these phantoms and let them go, we may discover a space, a break in the chatter, a glimpse of open sky. This is our birthright—the wisdom with which we were born, the vast unfolding display of primordial richness, primordial openness, primordial wisdom itself. All that is necessary then is to rest undistractedly in the immediate presence, in this very instant in time" (1997, pp. 106–7).

Suddenly I remembered what to do—rest in the immediate presence. I began resting between my in-breath and out-breath and I rested in between my anxious thoughts. I found that space to be vast, comforting and calming. I was called in for my X-rays and I continued to focus on the space in between my breaths. I brought curiosity to the moment and thought, "Isn't this all quite interesting?" as if it was a novel experience or discovery. After another wait, I was called into the ultrasound room. As I was getting positioned on the table, I noticed how nice it was to lie down and rest and I felt my body relaxing. I appreciated the kindness of the technician who was careful to make me feel at ease, and I felt compelled to send her lovingkindness ("may you be well, may you be at ease"). In those moments, I was fully present with what was unfolding. There was no resisting at that point; I recognized that the situation was completely out of my control. So, I did my best to rest in whatever spaces I could find.

Fortunately, this particular situation had a happy ending. These situations don't always release us from their grip, and then we need to dig deeper into our intrinsic sources of strength and resilience. We practice mindfulness with our everyday trials and tribulations so we can tap into our inner resources when the tornados of our lives touch down. We may not notice that our inner resources are being strengthened until they are put to the test. And then we understand fully how much our practice matters.

I often wonder what that experience would have been like without the serendipitous discovery of that email. Perhaps a different teacher or teaching would have arrived. Or perhaps I would have "failed the test" and collapsed into my fear and anxiety. The truth is that we are not going to always handle groundlessness as well as we would like. But we will always have new opportunities to bring mindfulness into these moments. If we are willing and open, we can let the uncertainty in our life become our teachers and guides.

Don't Know Mind

The certainty of uncertainty ensures that we will have a lifetime to practice working with groundlessness. We all know what uncertainty felt like when it took hold of our world in March of 2020 as the global pandemic washed over us. We confronted a new level of groundlessness and fear along with vast limitations on our freedom that we couldn't have imagined before the pandemic, not to mention the realities of illness, death, grief, loss and financial devastation. While the rug was pulled out from under us collectively, our individual experiences of the pandemic were wide ranging and diverse depending on our circumstances. From my privileged position of having a safe house to shelter in, a loving family to prevent the pain of isolation, the ability to work from home and the resources to cover my basic needs, I experienced groundlessness in a particular way. The very real disparities that many people faced, and the loss of loved ones, forced additional levels of groundlessness and suffering. But what we all shared in those moments was a complete and total lack of a reliable compass for our lives and the world.

While the pandemic has been an unusually large wave, these waves have always been washing over us and they will keep coming. When we think we've found stability, there is another wave to look out for. Life is slippery like that. And as much as we want to control what happens, we simply can't. A definition of suffering is *wanting things to be different than what they are.* So naturally, there is a lot of suffering that happens when we resist change. Just as there is no escape from change, we can't predict what will happen next.

There is a Taoist story that offers a helpful perspective on the nature of change.[7] It goes like this:

There was an old farmer who had worked his crops for many years. One day his horse ran away. Upon hearing the news, his neighbors came to visit. "Such bad luck," they said sympathetically.

"Maybe," the farmer replied.

The next morning the horse returned, bringing with it three other wild horses. "How wonderful," the neighbors exclaimed.

"Maybe," replied the old man.

The following day, his son tried to ride one of the untamed horses, was thrown, and broke his leg. The neighbors again came to offer their sympathy for what they called his "misfortune."

"Maybe," answered the farmer.

The day after, military officials came to the village to draft young men into the army. Seeing that the son's leg was broken, they passed him by. The neighbors congratulated the farmer on how well things had turned out.

"Maybe," said the farmer.

This story points to both the unpredictable outcomes of events and the freedom that comes from accepting that we don't know what will happen. When we bring the attitude of beginner's mind to our experience, we can remain open to the possibilities rather than constricted by our desires. As Shunryu Suzuki famously said, "In the beginner's mind there are many possibilities, but in the expert's mind there are few." Beginner's mind is not detachment. It's not "I don't care." It is a stance of openness to what is happening and availability to the vast set of possibilities that this moment and the next moment has to offer. In beginner's mind, predictions are useless. Labels and judgments are not helpful. There is only what is right now and how we relate to this moment. The rest we can't control.

There's a popular saying in Buddhist circles that I call upon when I'm managing my own feelings of uncertainty: *Right now, it's like this.* That's all I can know. The phrase brings me back to the present moment, gently reminding me that I am not in control of anything beyond how I relate to this moment, right now. Pema Chödrön offers the phrase *no big deal* to further put things into perspective. The beautiful moments and the painful ones all inevitably rise and fall to change. If we take the perspective of *no big deal*, we don't have to get caught up in attachment or aversion, blame or judgment. That doesn't mean we dampen the experience of joy or devalue our pain. But it implies that we can step out of the drama to see each moment for exactly what it is, part of the flow of our 10,000 joys and 10,000 sorrows. Remembering these pithy phrases can help us with perspective.

There is also a stance we can take in our mindfulness practice—strong back, soft front—that supports our attitude of being open to change. We can be readied and steadied for life with a strong back, employing the protections and boundaries that we need. At the same time, we can be open and available to what comes with a soft front. There is great flexibility in this stance which we practice in our sitting meditation when we settle into an alert and relaxed position, with an open and compassionate heart. The attitudes that we cultivate in meditation, like patience, trust, non-striving and curiosity, further support our flexible stance. These attitudes can help us steady and calm our minds and our hearts even as the world around us shakes. And mindfulness invites us to sit in the midst of it all, to rest in the ocean while the ocean heaves, as does the Little Duck in Donald Babcock's poem:

And what does he do, I ask you?
He sits down in it!
He reposes in the immediate as if it were infinity
which it is.
He has made himself a part of the boundless
by easing himself into just where it touches him.[8]

It is easy to feel a sense of equanimity in these words. In this repose of presence, fear has space to dissipate. Why? Because fear is a product of anticipating the future. When we are sitting present in a boundless sea of change, we are not anticipating a future challenge. Equanimity is a beautiful concept to contemplate. It represents that balance between being alert and relaxed with beginner's mind. It is the steadiness that comes from remaining centered in the middle of the heaving ocean. It is the space of "primordial wisdom" that Pema Chödrön describes. The calm abiding of equanimity is independent of external circumstances. It comes from accepting that the very nature of ocean, of life, is change.

The Fallacy of Control

More often than not, however, our minds do not calmly abide. There is a spectrum of attitudes that we might bring to moments of difficulty—from indifference and apathy to sheer resistance. Rather than sitting in repose while the ocean heaves, we might try to control the waves or ready ourselves for the blow. If there are too many difficulties tugging at us, we might give into the undertow. Our responses to uncertainty will be different based upon our conditioning and circumstances But, they are rarely born out of equanimity.

I was not raised with any real reference points for managing change. Most of us weren't. The concepts of acceptance and groundlessness were foreign and difficult for me to comprehend when I first immersed myself in Buddhist philosophy in college. While they became intellectually accessible over time, it has only been through the portals of change and difficulty in my life that I have been able to fully embrace the power of surrender.

I had learned to employ control to keep my emotions at bay as a young child, to manage my disappointments in life and to maneuver safely through my relationships. I always felt that if I couldn't control things and manage them perfectly then I was a failure. Worse, I feared I would get swept up in chaos and disarray. I put significant energy into my control strategies and my sense of self came to depend on my ability to look like I was steering my ship. I believed that others needed me to be this way, to see me in control. Nothing could be further from the truth. And nothing I did took me further away from my authentic self or more strongly fortified the wall of separation between myself and others.

I know now that I'm not the only person who spent my formative years practicing the art of control. Many of us are masters at control. But in our attempt to master control, control can master us. It has us hide behind our masks, covering up our true selves and severing our capacity to connect. The more we cling to our control strategies and how we want things to be, the more we have to protect, manage and defend.

And herein lies the myth of control. Not only do we never have it to begin with, but we create a reality that we find ourselves believing. Upholding the story of control allows us to believe we can wrestle stability from an unstable world. It prevents us from recognizing what's really happening and seeing things for how they really are—impermanent, everchanging and largely out of our control.

Learning to let go of the façade of control and to stay open to change has taken place for me in stages and phases. My mindfulness practice has led me to discover a part of myself that I affectionately call "Jabba the Hutt," who has revealed a lot to me about the pervasiveness of my control habits. Jabba is the intense, driven, goals-oriented part that keeps me busy, competitive and highly productive. When I am activated and Jabba is in control, I feel completely cut off from my natural ability to flow with the current of life. When I pay closer attention, I can see that what lies beneath Jabba is my fear of being seen as weak, ineffective and unworthy. Of course, what is under that is a fear of being unlovable.

There were times early in the pandemic that Jabba went into overdrive. So many things felt out of my control as the virus washed through our county. Jabba nudged me to work harder, teach more mindfulness classes, ramp up my community work and be as available for Aidan as possible. I had to look hard to see that I was struggling with the anxiety of groundlessness, and I desperately wanted to control the things in my life and around me that felt out of control. So, I fell again into my "comfortable" pattern of doing more.

This was not everyone's reaction to the lack of certainty that the pandemic brought. I watched as some of my colleagues and friends checked out on account of the uncertainty. I saw the panic of the situation drive people to hoard, steal and self-protect. I lost a friend to suicide after her relationship and business fell apart, and she found herself facing the idea of starting over. Control comes in all different shapes and forms, and it is shaped by a range of variables including beliefs, circumstance and conditioning. As I exhausted myself to make sure that I didn't have to feel the groundlessness that Jabba was trying to protect me from, I would remind myself of what I inherently knew—"Right now, it's like this." This would help me to momentarily unhand the things that I could let go of.

Tara Brach tells a story in her book *Radical Acceptance* about Mohini, a white tiger that lived in the Washington D.C. zoo. Mohini spent many years housed in a twelve-by-twelve-foot cage, pacing restlessly back and forth. When a natural habitat was built for her, the biologists and staff anticipated that Mohini would embrace her new environment. Instead, Mohini immediately settled into a corner of the compound, pacing until a twelve by twelve-foot area was well worn. That is where she remained for the rest of her life. As Brach writes, "Perhaps the biggest tragedy in our lives is that freedom is possible, yet we can pass our years trapped in the same old patterns... like Mohini, we grow incapable of accessing the freedom and peace that are our birthright" (2004, p. 25).

This doesn't have to be the case. Yet, the challenging circumstances in our lives can make our freedom seem out of reach. Recognizing our control strategies can be a fruitful part of our mindfulness practice as can be sending those parts of ourselves who are trying to protect us—like Jabba—some care and compassion. Among my students' favorite meditation practices is when we name our physical tension, our mental states and the clenching of our heart and we bow to the tight spots, thanking them for protecting us and letting them know that we're okay. We say to ourselves, "Thank you for trying to protect me. Thank you for trying to take care of me. I'm okay now. I'll be alright, thank you." It is such a compassionate practice to acknowledge the truth of our protective control patterns rather than admonishing them. We can let those parts of ourselves know that we can handle whatever arises. Sometimes we simply need a reminder that our freedom is there, waiting for us, when we're ready for it.

Staying Open and Present

As I described earlier, there are few things in our lives that force us to confront groundlessness more quickly than illness

111

and pain. When our bodies feel shaky or sick or we are given an unsettling diagnosis, we easily revert to strategies that help us seek steady ground. We tend to throw arrows at our struggle, pain or diagnosis, fueling the fires of our suffering. But there are other options.

Few meditation teachers have helped me understand this as clearly as Toni Bernhard. In her book *How to Be Sick* this longtime meditation practitioner describes the painful and complicated journey that she faced after finding herself with a mysterious, undiagnosable chronic condition that left her unable to get out of bed most days. Without any medical relief in sight, Toni was left to her own devices to learn how to live with her chronic illness. She called upon Buddhist wisdom and her meditation practice to help her step off of the wheel of suffering. She did this by intentionally cultivating mental states like lovingkindness, compassion, empathetic joy and equanimity in the midst of her pain. She practiced facing the difficulties rather than turning away.

Bernhard writes in closing that she learned to take refuge in the practices that were "waiting in the wings" to see her through (2018, p. 181). Staying present to her life, the way it was, not the way she wanted it to be, did not offer her freedom from her pain or relief from illness. But it allowed her to stand in the midst of the waves with an open heart in order to receive the many gifts that her life was offering when it would have been easy to turn away.

In *True Refuge*, Tara Brach describes how our false refuges of seeking relief rather than facing our pain are a common way we try to control our experience so that we don't have to feel our grief. As she surrendered to the grief brought about by her struggles with a rare genetic condition, she found that a quiet presence opened up allowing her to access unconditional love and compassion. As she writes, "The more I opened to this aliveness, the more I could sense an alert inner stillness, the background inner space of pure being. And the more I rested in that stillness, the more vividly alive the world became" (2012, p. 275).

As Brach suggests, letting go of our false refuges allows us to mourn our losses as part of our healing. As we mourn, we can become available to the ways that "love springs forth in our life." When we allow our suffering to be an object of exploration and a vehicle for true presence, we have an opportunity to inhabit the wholeness of our lives, regardless of our limiting circumstances. Unexpected sprouts of healing, growth and joy can emerge when we accept what is happening in our lives and we are not dependent on life being a certain way.

We tend to expect and rely on our medical institutions to make our pain go away. In our desperate plight for relief, we often forget that we can develop a different relationship to our pain and define the limits to our suffering. We seek medical cures when we are sick. But there often is healing, beyond the horizon of disease, that our hearts are longing for. When we live in the shadow of fear, feeding our control instincts or handing over control to others, our inherent wisdom remains hidden from view. Only when we surrender into life and let go of the hope for change, can we truly be free.

Waking Up from Denial

Denial is among the strongest types of control we exert to manage the discomfort of groundlessness. We have seen this most painfully in the politics of COVID-19 and global warming that have been strengthened through powerful discourses of denial. Denial marks how our culture deals with aging and death as entire industries have been built around the false pretense of eternal youth. Denial has been around for a long time. Acceptance is waiting for us to wake up, as the classic Buddhist story of the mustard seed illustrates.

As the story goes, a young woman in ancient India had lost her one-year-old son suddenly. Befallen with grief, she carried her dead son's body around the village looking for someone to help her save her child. A neighbor suggested she visit the Buddha who was camped near the village. When she showed Buddha her son's body and asked how to bring the boy back to life, the Buddha instructed her to return to the village, get a mustard seed from a villager who has not known death and bring it back to him.

The woman set out hopefully, knocking on the first neighbor's door. She shared her story and inquired if her neighbor had a mustard seed. When the neighbor presented a seed to her, she remembered to ask if the home had been touched by death. She listened as the neighbor shared his story of loss and grief. The woman set off to the next house. House by house, she learned of tragic losses, of children lost at childbirth, of loved ones passing away. As she learned that death was inevitable, she was able to acknowledge the truth of her own loss and she knew that she was not alone in her grief.[9]

I shared this story a few years ago while video recording a module for my Living Mindfully online program. After I concluded my thoughts on loss and acceptance, I looked up from the camera and found the videographer in tears. I asked her what about that story had touched her. She explained that her family lived in China, and she hasn't been able to travel to see them. She has a sick grandmother who she knows will be dying soon. She said, "My family hasn't been talking about how sick my grandmother is and I've felt like they don't care. But the story made me realize that maybe they are in denial or don't know how to talk about it. Maybe they do care. And maybe I need to let them know that we can talk about it and acknowledge what is happening." We may not realize how our denial affects others and how much healing can occur when denial is replaced with acceptance.

Recently, I led my students through a practice of the Five Remembrances, a teaching on impermanence that is chanted every day in most Theravadin Buddhist monasteries:

Breathing gently, I lovingly remember this body is aging.
Breathing gently, I lovingly remember this body is vulnerable
to illness.
Breathing gently, I lovingly remember this body will die.
Breathing gently, I lovingly remember that loss is part of life.
Breathing gently, I lovingly remember to meet this moment
with wisdom.

When we finished, I looked up at my Zoom screen filled with
boxes of thoughtful faces. I knew this was a big offering and I
let us collectively hold space for the words. One of my students
spoke into the silence and asked if that was meant to remind us
to live our lives fully. He was the optimist of the group, the one
that always reminded us that joy was but a moment away from
sorrow. "Yes," I replied. "And it is also an offering to wake us
up out of denial. The more we grasp onto our illusions, the more
we suffer. We can remember instead that change is a predictable
aspect of our lives. And freedom comes when we accept the
inevitability of change and loss." One of the students who was
mourning the recent loss of her mother privately wrote to me in
the chat box, "I really needed that. Thank you."

We may not recognize that peace can come when we stop
chasing relief. Frank Ostaseski, co-founder of the Zen Hospice
Project writes in *The Five Invitations*, about a homeless man,
Lorenzo, dying of lung cancer who came to hospice in a dark
place, expressing a wish to die. He was angry about being
forced to let go of the things he loved on account of his illness,
particularly walking in the park and writing in his journal. But
over the course of his three-month stay, as he was cared for and
given the space to express his fears, Lorenzo found that letting
go was workable. He came to see these activities as nothing
more than "chasing desire." Frank asked him if those activities
were no longer important. Lorenzo responded, "No it's not the
activities that bring me joy. It's the *attention* to the activities.

Now my pleasure comes from the coolness of the breeze and the softness of the sheets" (2017, p. 79).

Facing change, uncertainty and loss are never easy; we are hardwired to seek security and relief at all costs. But as Lorenzo attested, when we are willing to dive into reality, when we are not dependent on circumstances or outcomes, we can access the possibility of freedom and peace. Theravada Buddhist monk Bhante Henepola Gunaratana writes, "We spend all of our energies trying to make ourselves feel better, trying to bury our fears, endlessly seeking security. Meanwhile, the world of real experience flows by untouched and untasted. In mindfulness meditation we train ourselves to ignore the constant impulses to be more comfortable, and we dive into reality instead. The irony of it is that real peace comes only when you stop chasing it" (2011, p. 27).

Facing groundlessness can be difficult, particularly when it requires us to surrender control. But there can be a far higher cost to resisting the truth of change and uncertainty, particularly when we lock ourselves inside Mohini's cage. Instead, if we are willing to replace fear with acceptance, we can encounter a new world of possibilities, including the potential for greater peace. Surrendering in the face of groundlessness is a courageous act. It requires "a heart that is ready for anything" (Brach 2012, p. 279). As we will see in the next chapter, a present and open heart is the doorway to accessing what we need to stay steady, even when the ground below us falters.

***

Practice: Cultivating Acceptance in the Face of Uncertainty

Begin this practice by making an intention to be fully present in your body for these moments. Find a relaxed but alert seated position on your cushion or chair. Release the tension in your shoulders, feel your chest opening and inhale fully. Then release the breath slowly noticing the sensation of letting go. Allow your attention to scan through your body, noticing if there is any tension that wants to be released or areas of holding that want to let go. Sit quietly for a few moments feeling your breath as it rises and falls.

Now bring to mind a situation that is making you feel uneasy. This should not be a significant difficulty or trauma in your life but something that brings up feelings of uncertainty or feels unresolved. Notice what arises in your body when you bring this situation to mind. Perhaps you notice a sensation of tightness or tension, a fluttering in the stomach or a clenching of the heart. Once you've identified a sensation in your body, see if you can open up space for it. You may want to silently note, "This belongs, this too belongs." Maybe you want to note, "Everything changes, this too will change." Notice what happens when you open and welcome the sensations that arise with the feeling of uncertainty.

Staying open to the experience of groundlessness, with curiosity and kindness, can help to relax the tension that accompanies our natural resistance to uncertainty. With practice, you can notice the softening in your body and heart space and experience the gradual widening of your window of tolerance.

Chapter 7

Freeing Our Compassion Energy

It is this tender heart that has the power to transform the world.
—Chögyam Trungpa

Aidan woke up in a really happy mood one morning. During breakfast, he was singing about how much love he had for his family. He sang to our dog, "Chipper, you get 33% of my heart. Mom, you get 33% of my heart and Dad, you get 33%." My heart felt open that morning and I saw the perfect teaching moment. I said, "You know, you don't have to divide your love for us. You can offer Chipper every ounce of your love and you will have plenty left over for me and Dad. There's no limit." He looked at me with wide eyes. And something seemed to click. He turned back to our dog and said, "Chipper, you get 100% of my love and Mom and Dad can get the rest."

If only it is that easy to grasp the infinite availability of love. But most of us don't ponder how much love we have to give, or any aspect of our hearts at all. We don't tend to pay much attention to the feelings that amble through our heart space. We may feel those feelings profoundly when we are in the throes of romantic love or grieving love lost. But in between strong currents of emotion, the heart may simply be viewed as an anatomical entity existing to pump blood. This narrow view is not shared in all cultures. The word that ancient Egyptians used for happiness can be translated as "wideness of heart." Conversely, the translation for the word unhappiness is "truncated or alienated heart" (Doty, 2017, p. 246).

This concept of "alienated heart" seems to fit what ails our Western society. Our individualistic and materialistic culture has created the conditions for pervasive separation, loneliness and isolation. Western culture can still be likened to "a great uprooted tree with its roots in the air" as D.H. Lawrence (in Brach, 2004, p. 21) long ago described it. So, how do we deepen our connection with ourselves, others and the world around us? And what role does mindfulness play in cultivating a "wideness of heart"?

I recently experienced the power of presence and connection at a week-long family retreat in the Colorado mountains. After spending the mornings in organized activities, our kids were free to play all afternoon. Aidan quickly bonded with a pack of kids he had never met before. They ran wildly and joyfully for hours on end throughout the camp. They crafted a hide-and-seek game of epic proportions, hiding in lodges, cabins and tents and running through trees, bushes and grasses. Their time was not organized by scheduled sports, music lessons or errands. Nor was it engulfed by technology. I watched in awe as the simplest games were enacted with pure, unadulterated presence.

Watching this joy of freedom and connection was not the only valuable experience of camp. The kids were also being taught how to be present with their feelings. About midway through the camp, Aidan woke up in a super grumpy mood. I felt it permeate our space as we got dressed and ate breakfast. By the time we had settled in for our morning gathering, I was extremely annoyed and tense. "What is wrong with him?!" I asked myself. "What did I do wrong to raise such an unappreciative kid?" I was silently throwing arrows at Aidan and myself as we settled into our cushions. To my surprise, the instructor slowly looked around the room and asked, "Is anyone here feeling grumpy today?" I saw Aidan's hand slowly rise along with a number of other hands. I acknowledged that I, too, officially fit into the grumpy category, so I raised my hand. Julie then said, "How about this, what if we just sit here for a little while feeling our grumpiness?" And she rang the bell and led us into a moment of silence.

Within a moment I felt Aidan's body relax next to me. And then, as I opened to my frustration, I began to feel my tension melt. I was astonished at how quickly my mood shifted. Rather than continuing to throw arrows, I was given permission to relax *into* my discomfort. As Julie shared the itinerary for the day, Aidan leaned over to me and pointed to a two-year-old dancing in the front of the room with reckless abandon, his little jeans falling to his ankles. Aidan's smile was wide, his face was relaxed and his eyes were shining again. He was ready to begin his day. With the simple reminder that we are perfectly okay exactly how we are, we could both return to presence and connection.

It is easy to see how our "wideness of heart" can be obstructed and constricted given the complicated, overscheduled and divisive world that we live in. Without space to feel our hearts in all of their grumpiness and joy, we lose connection with our key source of nourishment. That connection is not to be taken for granted; cultivating a "present heart" is a necessary step for finding peace, equanimity and compassion within ourselves and in the world. Mindfulness goes far deeper than quieting the mind and stilling the body. Our practice helps us to tend to the heart, the ultimate source of connection and compassion.

Caring and Connection

In one of my meditation classes, a woman shared her deepest heartbreak with the group. She asked if we could hold her in our hearts the following week, for it was the 10-year anniversary of the death of her son who would have been 30. His was not a peaceful death, she explained. It was traumatic, and this fact made the upcoming anniversary even more painful for her. She said that she keeps returning to our meditation group because she is comforted and supported by the community. As she described, our weekly meetings offer her a space to both hold the pain and to take care of herself.

The space that we share in our sessions is rich with compassion, which comes naturally for this group. When the pandemic hit and I moved the classes online, the group found the support from each other more important than ever. One of my students recently told me that the classes were a lifeline during the early months of COVID-19; the group kept her hopeful and the teachings kept her focused when she was afraid that she would go into a downward spiral.

When someone is missing from class, the group inquires to find out how the person is doing. When someone in the group is ill, they seek updates and send well wishes. And whenever someone returns from having missed a class or two, we usually hear about how good it feels to reconnect with the group and with themselves. Our practice is to get quiet, settle into the breath and body and open to the waves, to whatever is present. The waves might be theirs alone as they sit in meditation. But we are sitting together, and we are well aware that we are holding space for each other. When someone speaks of their experiences out loud, they find that their waves are part of a larger ocean. We acknowledge the connection between us. The power of the meditation community, the sangha, cannot be underestimated. We may meditate alone but we are holding a larger space together.

Native cultures have long understood the healing power of holding space and revealing truths through collective ritual, as my meditation group has found in our practice together. Ceremonies and the symbols used to perform ritual are important in many cultures and religions for restoring harmony within the individual and community. Tara Brach (2004) shares a story told by author Michael Meade about an African tribe in Zambia that views an individual's illness as a sign that an ancestor's tooth has become lodged within that person. Unlodging the tooth is a community matter achieved by sharing truths. The sick person reveals their troubled feelings, and then all members of the tribe must also share their hurts for the full truth to come out. In this way, the cure for the individual's malady comes through the community's willingness to collectively name and heal their hurts.

In the U.S., we tend to seek more individual forms of healing, like mental health counseling from therapists and medical treatment from health providers. But research shows that the *relationships* we build with those who offer us care are critically important for the healing process. We know that when a therapist is mindful and attuned to the client, clinical outcomes are more positive than when these qualities are not present (Shapiro and Carlson, 2009). Experiencing genuine care, compassion and connection can heal. It can also decrease stress, boost the brain, increase resilience and fight loneliness (Jinpa, 2016).

We are often blocked from connection and the collective sources of healing that are available to us because of fear, shame or conditioned beliefs about our unworthiness or separateness. We may view our suffering as personal, something we caused, rather than seeing how our suffering can arise out of the conditioning that we have inherited from our families, caregivers and society (Brach, 2020). When suffering is viewed as ours alone, then we believe that it is a problem that only we can "fix" and we may close ourselves off from the help of others. Our sense of separation can make it difficult to receive the kindness of others and cross the bridge into people's lives.

Crossing the Bridge

Connection doesn't have to be complicated for it to be impactful. In fact, sometimes the simplest moments of care are the most powerful. I observed a beautiful example of connection a few years ago at a community event I attended. I was sitting next to a friend named Daniel. We were invited to greet the people sitting around us and both Daniel and I turned around to meet an older couple behind us. I noticed immediately that the woman seemed to be in great pain. She was holding her body in a guarded way and her face was tense. After we introduced ourselves, Daniel asked if the couple had been coming to the center for a while. The husband said it had been quite a while since they had been there. He pointed to his wife and said that they only come when she's feeling up to it. Daniel took the invitation and looked directly into the woman's eyes. With deep curiosity he asked, "And how are *you* feeling today?" She said she would give her day a "C." Daniel paused and nodded and said that he was glad that she felt well enough to join.

My eyes were drawn to this woman's necklace. On the chain was a silver disk with the words "fuck cancer" etched into the silver dome. When I looked up from her necklace and gave her a smile, I saw her look at me with eyes of defiance. I can still feel the intensity of that look. I sat down in my chair and was simultaneously overcome with appreciation for Daniel's kindness and compassion for the woman's plight. I was humbled to have experienced that moment of authenticity, and I wondered how many people would have stepped into it with such grace as Daniel did.

We don't often take the opportunity to cross the bridge into someone else's life. And we may not recognize how much we can benefit from those connections. This separation creates loneliness. And research shows that loneliness can be worse for our health than smoking 15 cigarettes a day (Yeginsu, 2018). The "loneliness epidemic" was a significant issue even before COVID-19. In 2018, nearly half of Americans reported that they sometimes or always felt alone. A 2021 report by the Harvard Graduate School of Education suggests that over one in three Americans now face "serious loneliness" (Weissbourd, et al., 2021).

There are a number of reasons that many of us are not comfortable walking across the bridge of compassion. Fear is the most prominent barrier to compassion. We may be afraid that caring will make us feel weak or vulnerable, that we will be taken advantage of, that we can't tolerate others' distress or we will feel too immobilized to be able to do anything to change the situation (Sood, 2013). We all know the impacts of these barriers. I can't count the number of times that I walked by a homeless person without looking up because I was afraid that my concern, fear or inability to substantially help would lead to an uncomfortable moment. As I have deepened my compassion practice and my commitment to supporting the dignity of all people, I now make an effort to look directly into the person's eye, to offer a warm smile of connection and to silently wish them well.

What we may not recognize is that compassion does not put us at risk of being taken advantage of and we can handle another's distress, as long as we develop healthy boundaries. Compassion is not about taking on someone's distress. As front-line workers, first responders, therapists and health providers know well, empathetic burnout is waiting to happen when we directly take on the suffering of others, particularly for long periods of time. But with awareness, we can deploy "rational" empathy where we can try to understand what another person is going through, but we step back and ask, "How can I help?" rather than enlisting ourselves to the task of fixing the suffering.

Elizabeth Gilbert provides a helpful distinction between empathy and compassion. In a 2020 TED Talk, she explained that empathy suggests, "You're suffering and now I'm suffering because you're suffering," whereas compassion says, "I'm not suffering right now, you are. I see your suffering and I want to help you."[10] Compassion includes the awareness of the suffering of another, and it involves an instinctive desire to see that situation relieved. But wise compassion knows boundaries. There are situations in which acting upon our desire to help is not physically or emotionally safe. In these cases, we can still act compassionately by wishing someone well, even if these well-wishes don't leave our lips.

Traditional lovingkindness practices are powerful in this regard. Lovingkindness is a practice that helps us cultivate feelings of goodwill by repeating traditional phrases wishing ourselves and others well. There are many different versions of this practice. We sometimes start by wishing ourselves well by repeating these phrases ("May I be well, may I be safe, may I be peaceful and at ease") and then we extend the caring to those we love, to neutral people, to those whom we dislike and those whom we don't know. Eventually we extend the caring to all beings.

We have to meet ourselves where we are in this practice. Sometimes it feels mechanical to repeat these phrases. Sometimes we feel strong resistance to wishing others well. For some of us, the hardest part of practicing lovingkindness is wishing ourselves well. This is why we sometimes start by sending well wishes to someone we love first, as this can be an easier starting point. A variation to the traditional practice is to then imagine that person wishing us well. If we can see our inherent goodness through the eyes of someone who loves us — a family member, a pet or even a deceased loved one — then we are more able to open up our hearts and wish ourselves well.

Brendon has inspired me to deepen my lovingkindness practice, as this has been something that I've long struggled with. But I've witnessed the impacts of his practice over the years as a deeper sense of peace has settled in. When Brendon hits walls in his relationships and doesn't have a direct path forward, he will practice lovingkindness daily, focusing on repeating special phrases for a particular person. So many of his difficult relationships have shifted *in his heart* because of his practice. He does not attempt to fix the things he cannot change. But he chooses not to keep his heart closed to the difficult people in his life.

Lovingkindness is powerful when practiced collectively, and I can always sense a palpable, kind feeling that is generated whenever I lead this practice. I always close my classes with a version of lovingkindness or compassion practice because I know how easy it is to take compassion out into the world once we've been saturated with it. Research demonstrates that lovingkindness meditation practices have both immediate and long-term impacts, including activating and strengthening areas of the brain responsible for positive emotions, compassion and wellbeing (Fredrickson et al., 2008; Davidson et al, 2003). We can intentionally train our hearts to open with kindness and caring. Moving out of the analytic mind with the help of a practice like lovingkindness can allow us to access the parts of ourselves that generate our natural capacity to care.

The Myth of Separation

Fear is not the only thing that holds us back from compassion and caring. We also hold back because of what Jack Kornfield (2009b) refers to as the "myth of separation." Particularly with the rugged individualism that is so prevalent in our culture, we are raised to believe ourselves to be separate from others. I own "my property," hold fast to "my beliefs" and covet "my ideas." Our materialistic culture reinforces the I-me-my-mine attitude while our political divide deepens our sense of separateness through rigid ideologies and beliefs. The more we sense ourselves as solid and separate the more we have to protect, support, defend and control. Our lives become more guarded and inflexible when our sense of separateness becomes the prevalent response to our underlying insecurities.

Beneath all of this lies a sense of inadequacy, self-limiting beliefs and perceptions that we are not enough. This thinking leads us to embrace a scarcity mentality where we operate from ideas like "since I don't have enough (time, money, love...) for myself, then I don't have enough to give." The myth of scarcity is just another story we tell ourselves. If we are willing to reframe this idea—like Aidan was able to do when I pointed out that he didn't have to divide up his love for me, his dad and our dog—then we can shift to an abundance mentality. When we make this shift, we can more easily tap into our generosity. And there is a generative quality inherent in generosity; it breeds more generosity. Moreover, we find ourselves to be more joyful when we focus on others, not on ourselves (Dalai Lama et al., 2016). In fact, giving without expecting anything in return can create natural stress relief (Brown, 2018).

We create separation when we live in a state of fear, when we experience greed and hatred and when we fall into ignorance. Each of these states creates suffering. Our loneliness gets exacerbated when we become contracted and self-consumed. Lovingkindness and compassion practices can help us move beyond our limited sense of self, break down the barriers of separation and widen our circle of care and connection.

Research shows that we are naturally empathetic. The brain's mirror neurons activate equally when we personally experience pain and when we see someone else experiencing pain (Sood, 2013). We inherently care about caring and we have a natural, built-in capacity for compassion. But when we are constricted on account of fear, unworthiness or a sense of separateness, our bridge toward the other, and our willingness to authentically connect, becomes severed. Our mindfulness, compassion and lovingkindness practices can help us repair that bridge.

Welcoming Self-compassion

Mindful awareness allows us to recognize the places where we are stuck, afraid and contracted. These places are fertile ground for self-compassion. We can begin to melt our protective shells when we bring some level of kindness to whatever we are feeling. As Pema Chödrön suggests, "[A]s we learn to have compassion for ourselves, the circle of compassion for others—

what and whom we can work with, and how—becomes wider" (2008, p. 120). We can't build that wider circle of care without self-compassion, which is our foundation for loving others. Yet our culture teaches us that being kind to ourselves is indulgent. So instead, we learn self-judgment, how to push ourselves hard and how to beat ourselves up when things don't pan out. Performance, achievement and competition is rewarded in our homes, schools and institutions, but not self-compassion. Selfless service is particularly reinforced for women in our culture. We are expected to give to others but not to ourselves.

Self-compassion can be learned. It requires that we first observe with mindful awareness how harsh and critical we are with ourselves. From there, we give ourselves permission to do things differently, to approach ourselves with kindness and gentleness. Self-compassion is a practice that may not come naturally at first. But over time it can become a natural response.

The power of self-compassion became evident to me a number of years ago after I picked up Aidan from his after-school program. He was having a rough week; he had been grumpy every day and we were finding ourselves regularly in a struggle. I decided earlier in the day that if another temper tantrum arose, I would come at it with compassion, recognizing that his struggles had nothing to do with me. As the energy began to escalate, I was preparing myself to silently practice lovingkindness and wish him well. But when the inevitable fuss and struggle came, I was surprised with my response. Rather than silently wishing him well, I paused in the moment that I felt myself getting triggered and I wished *myself* well. I took a minute, sat down, put my hand on my heart and acknowledged how bad I was feeling. There was a surprising amount of tenderness that came over me. I held myself for a long moment. The anger dissipated and I knew what I needed to do. I went to Aidan, gave him a big hug and told him I loved him.

Kristin Neff, a psychologist who researches self-compassion, points out the many ways that our culture negates its value; self-compassion is commonly viewed as self-pity, weakness, complacency, self-indulgence and selfishness. Instead, her research shows that self-compassion is linked to less self-focus, more strength, coping and resilience, more motivation and persistence, healthier behaviors and more generosity (Neff, 2012). The moment of care I gave myself not only helped me deescalate and recenter, but it led to a powerful moment of connection with Aidan. Taking time-out to shower myself with compassion was a far more productive approach than expressing the anger I felt, and it unexpectedly produced generosity of heart. When I teach others about self-compassion, I like to offer my students a reframe; that self-compassion is *self-full* rather than selfish. I have a lot of evidence in my own life to back this up. As I have found ways to take better care of myself, I have become a better mom, partner, co-worker and friend. It's just that simple.

Jon Kabat-Zinn offers a beautiful suggestion, a powerful image, that we can take into our practice, "you might try, just as an experiment, to hold yourself in awareness and acceptance for a time in your practice, as a mother would hold a hurt or frightened child, with a completely available and unconditional love" (2005, p. 163–4). When we do sitting meditation or recite lovingkindness phrases or do any number of compassion practices, we can put our hand on our heart to feel a physical connection with ourselves. HeartMath studies posted on their website point to a direct connection between the heart and the brain; the messages we send ourselves can be profoundly impactful energetically, neurologically and biochemically. Small acts of compassion are where we start. But we first need to give ourselves permission to welcome these expressions of care into our lives.

Catalyzing Compassion for Others

The process of opening our hearts toward ourselves and others is not always direct or linear. It may happen over time as we deepen our lovingkindness and compassion practice. But it will probably happen in fits and starts, with setbacks, forgetfulness and doubt. And sometimes compassion is cracked open when we least expect it. I've shared the story about Tom in my classes. Tom was a meditation practitioner who had come to one of Jack Kornfield's retreats. Jack describes how Tom had been feeling anxious during this retreat. His wife had recently been diagnosed with Parkinson's and Tom wasn't sure how to make sense of it. So, Jack suggested that Tom write a letter to himself to articulate what might be hidden from his awareness and then meditate on it for a few days. In doing so, Tom recognized his fear and insecurity and how shaky and confused he was.

As Jack described, "And when he brought his letter in and read it to me, he came alive. He began to feel his inner experience, all that was tumultuously going on in there, with greater honesty and clarity, because he took the time to begin to pay attention and listen and name it. He was beginning to trust that awareness could tune in to his feelings. But as he opened, his sense of suffering also increased—his wife's difficulties, the sufferings of other people, the Parkinson's patients in the clinic where he took her. The other illness and insecurity in the world became visible to him. And then he began to experience a welling up, not just of fear, but of compassion. And a kind of relief broke through him with that compassion" (2019b, p. 4).

After sharing the story in class, one student asked me, "Does it always happen that way? Does moving from mindful awareness to compassion happen naturally?" I asked what was driving her question. She explained that she's been taking care of her ill sister and rather than compassion, she feels a strong current of resentment. She wanted to burst open her well of compassion, as Tom did, but she didn't know how.

I acknowledged that her question, and her struggle with not feeling compassionate, obviously came from a deep place of compassion. And I shared with her some of the barriers to compassion that we naturally face. I encouraged her to continue practicing lovingkindness, both toward herself and toward her sister. And to be gentle to herself. The truth is that compassion is not always available to us when we'd like it and in the form in which we'd like it to be. We can't cajole it out of ourselves or force it into existence. We need to free the energies of compassion that naturally exist within us by gradually opening our hearts. We need to bring awareness to our resistance to compassion and resolve to open our hearts when we are ready. In order to do this, we need to stay awake and trust that our heart is already gentle and kind. We need to reconnect with what is already there and cultivate our kind qualities of heart.

Freeing Compassion Energy

When we can free the compassion energy that naturally exists in our hearts, we have enormous capacity to offer our care. However, this too requires wise discernment, less we risk burning out or offering compassion for the wrong reasons. A few months into the pandemic, I taught a class called Healthy Compassion. Given the complex set of needs we were seeing in our communities, I wanted to explore how we could all be of service during this time of crisis while at the same time caring for our own needs and staying physically and emotionally safe. I wanted to teach compassion in a way that didn't reinforce the selfless service mentality that was easy to latch onto in times of crisis but rather open up space for exploring how to participate in caring for *both* our hurting world and for ourselves.

I had my students take a self-assessment that examined their motivations in compassionate actions they recently undertook along with their perception of their current life balance, the reactions of others to their generosity and how they felt when they helped (Svoboda, 2013). Many of these actions, we learned, were driven by feelings like guilt and fear, particularly when they were not in a resourced and balanced place This was eye opening to them, along with the concept that their own wellbeing matters when they care for others, even (or especially) during a crisis time like a pandemic.

Many of us operate from the assumption that the world needs fixing so badly that we need to jump into helping headfirst. The world indeed needs fixing, but our mindfulness practice can help us see that those actions must come from a stable and resourced place and within healthy boundaries and self-awareness. As Clarissa Pinkola Estes, an American writer and psychoanalyst, writes, "Ours is not the task of fixing the entire world all at once, but of stretching to mend the part that is within our reach."[11] It is a wise compassion that guides us to know what to do, how, when and how much.

Cultivating self-compassion and extending compassion outwardly is critically important for our individual and collective wellbeing. We are deeply interconnected as a species and a planet, as both the pandemic and impacts of global warming have demonstrated. We can credit compassion for enabling our survival through our crises and trials, since the beginning of time. Evolutionarily, compassion has protected our vulnerable offspring, allowed us to cooperate with non-kin and help others (Weiss, 2018). Compassion continues to be essential to our physical and mental wellbeing. It helps us reduce negative mind states like anxiety, depression and stress, while increasing positive mind states like life satisfaction, connectedness, self-confidence and optimism (Neff, 2012). We also know that opening our hearts strengthens our sense of aliveness and resilience (Dalai Lama et al., 2016).

But there are guardrails. As we widen our circle of care for others, repeating the "Great Vow for Mindful Activists" can help remind us not to burn out:

Aware of suffering and injustice, I, ____, am working to create a more just, peaceful, and sustainable world. I promise, for the benefit of all, to practice self-care, mindfulness, healing, and joy. *I vow to not burn out* (Ikeda, 2020).

The energy of our compassionate heart can be freed. We don't have to live "like a great uprooted tree with its roots in the air," as D.H. Lawrence described. We can learn to relate to ourselves and to others with authentic loving presence. And we can build our capacity for "heartfulness" as we practice crossing the bridge toward others with compassion. Freeing our compassion energy requires us to continually pause, attune and relate to our moments with full presence, as Aidan and I were able to do that morning of family camp. As we deepen our mindful awareness, the energy of lovingkindness can be more easily freed.

As we develop the two wings of mindfulness—awareness and compassion—we see their impacts naturally ripple out in all directions. I've noticed the manifestation of mindfulness in the most ordinary, mundane moments. I can no longer drive by a dog on the loose without helping to find its home or forget to reach out to a friend or neighbor who is struggling with illness or loss. Brendon has made it a practice to leave a $5 gift to the person behind him on the occasions he drives through a coffee hut, insisting that it might change the course of that person's day. He recently bought a bumper sticker for his car that says, "I hope something good happens to you today." These may be small things in the grand scheme of life, but small actions matter. We attend to what is within our reach. One action builds on the next. Our moments of collective caring can produce magnificent winds of change.

It may not be easy to maintain our mindfulness practice when we feel like things are coming apart. But these are exactly the moments that call for mindfulness and compassion. These are also the moments in which our tender hearts are most able to feel the collective pain of others. When we stop to feel our own struggles, we can sense most acutely the struggles of others. If we can release the grip of fear, and step across the bridge, our caring for others can help to break down the great wall of separation and mend our collectively alienated heart.

Mindfulness is profoundly forgiving. When we stray off the path, we can simply come back to the beginning, back to presence. We can pause, take a breath and return to awareness in the moment. We can remember the attributes of acceptance, non-judgment, patience and trust. We can release the stories and open to the waves, with a strong back and soft front. As we continue to release, we may see new things that are obstructing our path. With our steadiness of heart, we can befriend whatever we find. "This too belongs," we can remind ourselves. We simply remember that all of it belongs, that all of our obstacles are part of our path toward cultivating greater calm, stability and an open heart.

***

Practice: The Gift of Lovingkindness

Take a moment to find a comfortable seated position on your chair or cushion and take a few full deep breaths. You might gently scan your mind and body. Notice what is present and what wants to be released or let go.

Tune into your heart for a moment and open your awareness to the feelings you've been carrying: the joy, the worry, the fear, the longing. Sense the state of your heart and how much it has been carrying.

Putting your hand on your heart if that is comfortable, you might silently repeat these phrases of lovingkindness:

May I be well

May I be free from fear

May I be safe from inner and outer harm

May I be at peace

Or you might select whatever words are resonant for you in this moment.

When you're ready, continue the practice by bringing someone to mind that can use healing attention right now. Sensing what it might be like for that person, repeat these or other phrases of lovingkindness for this person:

May you be well

May you be free from fear

May you be safe from inner and outer harm

May you be at peace

For the next few moments, you might bring several other people to mind that would benefit from your care and wishes, silently repeating these phrases for them:

May you be well

May you be free from fear

May you be safe from inner and outer harm

May you be at peace

Continue the practice, widening the circle of compassion as far as you'd like. When you have finished your wishes, you might put your hand on your heart and sit quietly, feeling the energy of compassion that has been released.

Conclusion

May you listen to your longing to be free.
—John O'Donohue

After the fraught year of 2020 came to a close, I came across an interview with Andean Medicine Man, Puma Fredy Quispe Singona, who was asked why we are going through the pandemic crisis. He responded that we took our freedom for granted until a global process took that freedom away. He suggested that we can reclaim our freedom, but we will need to learn how to use it more wisely. We will need to prioritize what is important and how to take care of ourselves and then we can take care of our family and community. Our task is to learn how to use our freedom more wisely so that we can be of service.[12]

Many wisdom teachers have responded to the question: Why do we suffer? Buddhist traditions offer time-tested principles and practices for working with and freeing ourselves from unnecessary suffering. The fundamental question we are asked to consider is: What do I want my freedom for? The pandemic was a type of litmus test for many of us in this regard. On the most basic level, the shut-down forced us to give up a lot of our liberties—to freely interact with others, to be in physical contact with loved ones, to go about our day-to-day business in the world, to feel safe. These were freedoms that many of us had previously taken for granted. As they became available again many people questioned if they want to return to their "old" ways of being. The pandemic initiated a massive re-evaluation of values and life choices.

But there is a deeper level of freedom that is alluded to here, that is not based on or constrained by our circumstances. It is the freedom that comes from recognizing and waking up from our habits, blind spots and ignorance. It comes from seeing, and transforming, the conditioning that gets locked into place in the absence of mindful awareness. As we inhabit this awareness, little by little, we begin to let go of our control impulses, fear-based grasping and the small-self we occupy to protect ourselves. As a result of our mindfulness practice, we can begin to see ourselves, our lives and the world more clearly, with fewer clouds of illusion blocking our view. When we live from a place of authenticity and clarity, we can, arguably, be of greater service to the world.

This book has explored a number of obstacles that naturally arise when we embark on our mindfulness journey and open to the possibilities of this freedom. It examines how accepting and leaning into these obstacles can lead to the awareness, wisdom and compassion we seek. Through personal stories and wisdom teachings, I have shared how even the most seemingly mundane moments can present life's most powerful lessons. Conversely, these examples illustrate how suffering is created when we reject and resist what shows up at our doorstep.

Our ability to work with our difficulties and find the truths hidden beneath our conscious awareness can help us manifest the inner resources that we so desperately need—the insight, compassion and resilience that can light the way through difficult times. We are fortunate to have access to wisdom traditions and teachings from across the globe that offer an abundance of tools for developing these resources. Yet, tools are of little use to us if we don't put them into daily practice as there is no shortcut to directly experiencing the teachings. Our realization of mindfulness may begin on an intellectual level, but it can only be fully embraced and experienced through its application in our everyday lives. Every waking moment is an opportunity to apply mindfulness. Regularly returning to the question, "What do I want my freedom for?" can help to keep us on the path.

Limitations of Mindfulness

Mindfulness is a powerful tool for helping us to wake up. But the practice of mindfulness is not a panacea. It won't make our problems go away, resolve our pain, banish our neuroses or dissolve our mistakes. Meditation won't lead most of us to permanent inner peace or make us perpetually kind and likable. As much as I can attest to the power of mindfulness, I am living proof of its limitations. I still get triggered, anxious and reactive. I act mindlessly and selfishly. I shut down and turn away. I indulge my old patterns of behavior. But I am well-aware of all of this now. I'm not at war with my neuroses. Our relationship has changed. I observe them and learn new things. I can drop the judgments and get on with my day. I am more caring for myself and compassionate with others. Mindfulness is not a cure-all for our personal or global problems. It is a mirror to help us see ourselves more clearly so that the thoughts and actions we put into the world can come from a wiser and more attuned place.

Mindfulness is just one of many helpers along the path, as the stories of my personal journey attest. I've benefited from a number of supportive modalities from psychotherapy to acupuncture which have been powerful and important adjuncts to my mindfulness practice. I have come to understand that there are times when we need to call on a professional team to support our work in releasing the obstacles that keep us trapped in cycles of suffering. We sometimes make the mistake of believing that meditation can heal all wounds when in fact it can exacerbate them, as those suffering from trauma may well know (Treleaven, 2018). There are particular difficulties that necessarily require other levels of professional support. We need to cultivate and accept a diverse toolkit for probing our symptoms and healing our pain.

While it is not a panacea, the mindful awareness we cultivate can serve as a compass for helping us navigate our lives and it can direct us toward what it is we need. As our self-awareness grows, so too can our confidence strengthen in our capacity to live as a force for the good. But like all navigation tools, mindfulness only points us in a particular direction. We are not escorted through the ports and doors of our lives. And we are fallible and distractable with plenty of room for navigating error. This truth was embarrassingly highlighted by an unfortunate recent event.

It was really bad timing. I pulled into a tight parking spot at the same time that the driver was opening his car door. My front bumper caved in like aluminum foil. I called my insurance company who recommended that I call the police. When I let the young driver know, he asked me to not make the call and proceeded to show me a picture of his 9-day-old baby while informing me that he didn't have a valid driver's license. My empathy kicked in, I put down my phone and he asked that I put his girlfriend's name down as the driver on my insurance paperwork, instead of him. I drove away, saddened by this man's predicament, and perplexed that I felt responsible to protect him. I filled out the online police report based on this story, hit submit and was instantly stunned by what I had done.

After hashing out the situation with a number of people I trusted who all agreed that I needed to confess the truth, I headed to the police station to determine the consequences. With great relief, I learned that the form I filled out was not actually a police form; it was filed in the revenue department. (Perjury charge avoided!) And, because the driver's car was parked when the accident happened, it didn't matter who claimed to be sitting in the driver's seat. He was safe. I was safe. I was relieved. And embarrassed. How could I have gotten so twisted up about how to handle this situation?

The incident impacted me greatly. I recognized that sometimes our intentions for compassionate action can be simultaneously virtuous and misguided. Perhaps this was a case of idiot compassion. But it hasn't deterred me. While I still haven't fixed the bumper, I have let go of the shame that I associated with the situation. Now, I simply allow the twisted bumper to remind me of how messy and imperfect our actions can be despite *or* on account of our best intentions. And I remember the promises *and* challenges of mindfulness that can arise simultaneously as we seek to lead our lives from the heart of compassion.

Four Truths

Fender benders, along with other life challenges, have the ingredients necessary to produce suffering. I threw dozens of arrows in those hours between the accident and my visit to the police station. In fact, my anxiety about the situation created such an energetic force in my house that Chipper became ill. The arrows I threw didn't just affect me, but they had a domino effect, as tends to happen with our reactivity. We all forget about mindfulness. Our compass gets muddy.

In times like these, I return to the wisdom of the Four Noble Truths, which are as simple as they are profound:

1. Suffering is part of life;
2. Suffering comes from how we relate to life and the amount of resistance, aversion, and grasping we attach to the way we want things to be;
3. Suffering is a symptom of our ignorance and delusion which we can overcome; and
4. There is a path that can help us end suffering and it involves, among other things, developing wisdom, practicing mindfulness and following a series of moral guideposts.[13]

The Four Noble Truths have long served as both a diagnosis and treatment for our afflictive and difficult times. The power of this teaching is beautifully reflected in a story that Jack Kornfield (2019a) shares about his teacher, Ajahn Chah, who was walking along the alms round in the morning with the monks when he sees a huge boulder in the field. He asks, "Monks, is that boulder heavy?" And of course, the monks say, "Yes, master, it is." He smiles and says, "Not if you don't pick it up."

We have a choice about whether or not to pick up the boulder, to increase our burden. It's tempting and instinctual to pick it up. But we can pause and ask ourselves: Do I want this burden, or should I keep on walking? In *Man's Search for Meaning* (1985), Viktor Frankl writes, "Everything can be taken from a man but one thing: the last of the human freedoms — to choose one's attitude in any given set of circumstances, to choose one's own way." It is powerful to recognize the freedom that is waiting for us depending on how we choose to relate to our circumstances. And when we get off course, it is empowering to know that we can take a breath and start again.

Not picking up the boulder goes against our hardwiring. Sometimes choosing to pick a fight, "fix" someone else's problem or indulge in our misery is more fun or familiar than letting go or letting be. Freedom from suffering alludes us not only because we are comfortable with our misery, familiar habits and stories but also because we don't see our unconscious patterns, the seeds of negativity we plant, our unskillful mental states or the laws of cause and effect. We don't see how we get caught by fear, attachment and aversion or how we act out in anger, desire, frustration, pride and self-pity. This is what is meant by ignorance and delusion, the root cause of our suffering according to the Four Noble Truths.

Thich Nhat Hanh (1997) suggests that we all have the capacity for awakening to these truths. We have what he calls "store consciousness" in which seeds are buried deep within the "soil of our consciousness," above which are "many, many layers of suffering, confusion, prejudices and so on." Our intellect covers over these seeds. He argues that our intellect can never go deep enough, and that, in fact, our intellect can often contradict our deepest nature.

We rely on our intellect to make sense of ourselves and the world. Our evolved prefrontal cortex allows us this luxury. However, our thinking mind leads us to false beliefs—that we are responsible for others, that we are unworthy of love, that we are defined by the pain and anxiety we experience, that we need to pick up the boulder rather than letting it be. Our intellect takes us into rabbit holes of shame, blame, hatred and greed. It blocks us from seeing how we get caught by our conditioning, passed down and through familial, generational and societal systems. Our thinking mind traps us in a small-self perspective, blocking the larger view of who we are. It convinces us that we are separate and alone.

Our mindfulness practice can help us shift out of the analytic mind so we can listen to other instruments of knowing, like our bodies and hearts. It helps us touch into the deeper places within us and the parts that get forgotten and left behind when we get hurt, grow up, get busy and solidify our identities. The veils of illusion can fall away as we train our attention inward. We begin to see how we get caught in our fear, aversion and attachments and the habits that get hardwired into our brains. As we begin to see more clearly, we can bring curiosity rather than animosity to our obstacles, for they are an integral part of the path. We start to see how these obstacles have worked in our lives and how they might be workable moving forward. As we learn to trust our inherent wisdom, we can begin to find our way back "home."

Basic Goodness

I use the word "learn" quite a bit in this book, as if we don't already know how to pause, breathe, attune to and befriend the difficulties and changes. The more appropriate word to use is "remember." We know how to be present, connected and compassionate. We don't begin as infants locked in an adversarial relationship with life. We learn how to protect ourselves in a world that doesn't always feel safe and accommodating. Mindfulness is a form of remembering—how to stay present, open and available in the moment, how to recognize who we really are, how to uncover our "deepest nature" and how to attain freedom from suffering.

Different Buddhist traditions give our "deepest nature" various names. Chögyam Trungpa Rinpoche described it as "basic goodness: as a fundamental openness, wisdom, compassion, and strength of mind and heart" (Nyima, 2020). The Dalai Lama refers to it as "Buddha-nature," our potentiality which is present but obscured by our delusions. Jack Kornfield describes Buddha-nature as our inner perfections, the qualities of the heart which include generosity, morality, lovingkindness and equanimity.

This concept of basic goodness, that we are already whole and complete, wise and stable, is not intrinsic to our culture. In fact, many in the West inherit a very different conception of self, ripe for the indoctrination of insecurity and a sense of unworthiness. When Sharon Salzberg famously asked the Dalai Lama what he thought about self-hatred, he was perplexed. What does this mean, self-hatred? he asked. How could one think of themselves in that way? In his homeland of Tibet, there is a fundamental understanding that everyone has the seed of Buddha-nature within us, waiting to be watered, ready to grow. For many in the West, it is difficult to comprehend this basin of love that exists within and for us but, as Salzberg (2002) suggests, it is "something we must nurture, since it's the foundation for being able to truly love and care for others."

Many people come to meditation because they feel faulty, unlovable and incomplete. As our practice melts away our layers of judgment, attachment to who we think we should be and aversion toward ourselves, we come to find that we are already whole and complete, that our "goodness" may just need a little dusting off. There is a classic story about the golden

Buddha that highlights the truth of our inherent goodness. In the late 1950s, a Thai monastery was being relocated by a group of monks. They were moving a giant clay Buddha statue when one of the monks noticed a crack. There was a golden light emanating from the crack. So, the monks chipped away at the clay until they found that underneath the clay was a statue made from solid gold. Historians believe that the statue had been covered in clay several hundred years earlier to protect it from an attack by the Burmese army. All of the monks had been killed and the gold remained hidden from view for hundreds of years.

This story is a beautiful reminder of what is eternal within us. Regardless of how many layers we use to cover up our pain, vulnerability, conditioning and insecurities, our gold remains accessible when we are ready to remove the covering. As I have experienced over my two decades process of "undoing," we can release our grip on the identities that we spend a lifetime constructing. In doing so, we begin to see ourselves as larger than our parts. Recognizing our gold, we can free ourselves from the cage of mistaken identities. Through our practice, we become less and more at the same time. As singer, songwriter and meditator Leonard Cohen once said, "the less there was of me the happier I got."

Hearing Our Song

Mindfulness offers one of many paths that can help us remember our true nature. Its principles are shared by many cultures across the globe. A few years ago, I attended a Bone Throw ceremony with a Peruvian Ka Ta See shaman and I was surprised to hear echoes from the mindfulness teachings I was so familiar with. For tens of thousands of years, the Ka Ta See has read from animal bones they collected. The animal spirits who inhabit the bones answer questions asked by the shaman to help the receiver on his or her path. This ancient form of divination is intended to help seekers recognize their "song," their true self. As the shaman, JoAnne, explained, our "song" can only be found when we remove our "mask" or the "face we wear to protect ourselves or hide our own truths." In the process of shedding our mask, we move closer toward remembering and reclaiming our "song."

JoAnne explained that our limiting beliefs and habitual patterns hold us back on our journey toward our song. Our struggles to overcome these barriers are "the doorways back into balance." The practice of letting go—of the limiting beliefs, mistaken identities, whatever is not serving our true self—is the key to opening these doorways. Letting go requires that we stay aware of what is called for in this moment and remain willing to shed unneeded layers of the past, to continue to align with our authentic selves. In closing the ceremony, JoAnne said, "Your healing is rooted in deep clarity for seeing yourself for who you really are" (Dodgson, 2019).

Universal teachings of our inherent wholeness have been transmitted by Buddhist teachers, shamans and medicine men alike, across a range of cultures, traditions and religions. The teachings help us to remember who we are when we are wandering through our lives disconnected from our true selves. In Shamanic traditions, our souls may need to be retrieved in order to return to our wholeness. Buddhist traditions encourage emptying the mind through long stints of silent meditation to come home to our true nature. But our remembering can happen in other ways; we might play with our child, connect with a loved one or listen to music, and we remember our song. Any moment of mindfulness is a step along the path back home.

When Aidan was young, we read him *Quiet Bunny* (2015) by Lisa McCue. The book is about a bunny who loves the sounds of the forest but believes that every animal except for himself has its own special sound. Quiet Bunny doesn't know how to find his sound. He mimics the other animals, unsuccessfully, until a wise owl advises him to "be whooooo you are, and you will find your own bunny sound." Bunny searches deep inside of himself to figure out what his unique sound is. Only after deep reflection did Bunny find his Thump in the forest. When he shared his thumping, the others joined in, and the sweet melody was richer than before. As Quiet Bunny finds, our coming home is part of a coming together, of recognizing our interconnectedness, that our song is part of a larger melody. As we access our wholeness, a greater sense of belonging becomes possible.

Many people begin on the mindfulness path with the goal of self-improvement. We expect that mindfulness will make us more happy, likable, successful, powerful or profitable. If we practice in earnest, we indeed experience changes. As Richard Davidson's groundbreaking research shows, we can see changes in the brain that impact emotion regulation (Spoon, 2018). We become more self-confident and kinder, as the Dalai Lama (2020) has long pointed out. Our productivity, focus and workplace efficiency become strengthened, as research on global corporations suggests (Houggard, 2019). There is no shortage of research and influential voices helping to keep us motivated on the path with inspiring stories. But if we stick to our practice, there may be other perfectly mundane and compelling experiences along the way. We may stop wanting to be anything other than who we are. Our longing for things to be different might drop away. Our hearts may feel a little bit softer. We may hear the soft notes of our song. We might tap into a deeper sense of belonging.

The Medicine We Need

There may well be a million paths up the mountain toward seeing ourselves clearly. There are endless spiritual traditions and practices that can help us remove the obstacles in our way to hearing our song. But there is no shortcut, only the testing out and trying on of wisdom so generously passed down generation after generation. We can open up our senses and feel what resonates within us. And then we can follow the call, however that process looks for us.

Our journey may not lead us directly to what it is that we desire, whether that be enlightenment, serenity or freedom from pain. But it will surely keep leading us back to our breath, back to presence, back to our heart. I return often to what Aidan shared with me as we were beginning our journey together through the pandemic lockdown: "You know how people say that there is no way around things, only through them? That's not true. When I'm doing a maze on paper and can't find my way out, I just start at the end point and work my way back to the beginning." I appreciate this approach; we indeed have the wisdom available within and around us to find our way back to the beginning, to the pause, the breath, the stillness of the present moment.

Even as the waves crash around us—as it feels they continuously do these days—we can take our seat and find the calm we need to navigate through rough waters. A larger perspective can come into view as the pain, grief or angst can recede to the background. Tara Brach (2013) shares the story of Tibetan teacher Chögyam Trungpa opening a class by drawing a V on a large white sheet of poster paper. He asked those present what he had drawn. Most responded that it was a bird. "No," he told them. "It's the sky with a bird flying through it."

When we see the open sky, we recognize what we already know to be true; that we are the open, wakeful awareness of the sky, through which the pain, anger or grief travels and dissipates. And as the book's opening story about the tranquil bird sitting on the ledge in the midst of the roaring waterfall suggests, our peace is already here, just waiting to be noticed. Catching glimpses of these truths can help us remember that wakefulness and peace are not dependent on our circumstances. Our present, stable heart is a breath away, even in the midst of storms. Remembering this can not only influence our individual lives but it can have a profound impact on those around us. As Thich Nhat Hanh explained: "When the crowded Vietnamese refugee boats met with storms or pirates, if everyone panicked, all would be lost. But if even one person on the boat remained steady and calm, it was enough. It showed the way for everyone to survive."[14]

The medicine that the world needs right now is more mindfulness, more compassion and more "present hearts." When we live from our wholeness, we can weather the storms and help others do the same. We can know the steps needed to help relieve our own suffering and the suffering of others. In sum, we can be a force for the good.

I asked Aidan a few years ago how he helps his heart to keep growing bigger. He responded, "I try to put as much good in the world as possible. Everybody makes mistakes, so if you just focus on the good and not get wound up about being perfect, I think that's how you help your heart to grow bigger." His message is simple enough: we focus on the good and let go of the rest. Jack Kornfield shares in *A Path with Heart* (1993) a powerful truth that the legendary Yaqui Indian Sorcerer don Juan offered to Carlos Castaneda in *The Teachings of Don Juan*: "Does this path have a heart? If it does, the path is good; if it doesn't, it is of no use."

We don't have to wait until the end of our lives to use our freedom wisely. We can begin now. We can pay a little more attention in *this* moment. We can quiet our busy mind, turn toward our emotions, open our hearts a little bit wider. We can be forgiving of ourselves when we make mistakes and offer others some grace and compassion. If all else fails, we can simply remember to pause and breathe. Perhaps we can learn from our kids and grandkids, the ones who understand the effortlessness of life, who don't question their gold, unencumbered by years of social conditioning. Aidan once shared a profoundly simple experience that stuck with me: "One time I was playing football with my friends and one of them did a cheap shot, but instead of getting mad, I just took a deep breath and we kept on playing." (He apologized, by the way.)

We can't prevent people from being unkind, align our circumstances to our favor or make our difficulties go away. But we can choose how we respond to life's cheap shots. And when we inevitably get activated, we can remember to take a deep breath and wish ourselves well. Our response in the moment matters. It is the generative action from which everything else follows, for better or for worse. One mindful thought, one kind action, when taken with full awareness, is how we craft our future, a wiser, more compassionate future that is fully and completely in our hands to shape.

Endnotes

1. Story adapted from Fronsdal, G. (2014) 'Tranquility as a Factor of Awakening', *DharmaSeed.org* [Podcast]. 1 January. Available at https://sr.dharmaseed.org/talks/21898/ (Accessed 3 July 2022).

2. See Akomolafe, B. (n.d.) *A Slower Urgency: We Will Dance with Mountains* [Online]. Available at https://www.bayoakomolafe.net/post/a-slower-urgency (Accessed 12 May 2021).

3. In Lion's Roar Staff (2018, March). 'Pema Chödrön & k.d. lang talk Buddhism, creativity, and "gapaciousness," *Lions' Roar,* 23 March [Online] https://www.lionsroar.com/pema-chodron-k-d-lang-talk-buddhism-creativity-and-gapaciousness/ (Accessed on 21 November 2021).

4. I address wise discernment throughout the book as it relates to bringing mindfulness to our difficulties, particularly when we have a history of trauma. See Chapter 5 for suggestions and approaches for working within our window of tolerance. For a comprehensive exploration of trauma-sensitive mindfulness, see Treleavon (2018).

5. From Mumford, G. (2017) 'Leading with wisdom,' *Transcript of Live Recording for Mindfulness Meditation Teacher Certification Program,* Louisville, Sounds True.

6. For a comprehensive exploration of research on the impacts of meditation on the brain, see Goleman & Davidson (2017) *Altered Traits: Science Reveals How Meditation Changes Your Mind, Brain, and Body*, London, Penguin Books.

7. See Ambler, C. (2015) *Zen Story: Maybe* [Online] Available at https://thedailyzen.org/2015/03/20/zen-story-maybe/ (Accessed on 18 August 2022).

8. Mindfulness Association (n.d.) *The Little Duck* [Online]. Available at https://www.mindfulnessassociation.net/

words-of-wonder/the-little-duck-donald-babcock/ (Accessed on 22 August 2022).

9. Story adapted from Siegel, R. D. (2009) *The Mindfulness Solution: Everyday Practices for Everyday Problems*, New York, The Guilford Press.

10. Gilbert, E. (2020) It's OK to feel overwhelmed. Here's what to do next. *TED Connects* [Podcast] 2 April. Available at https://www.ted.com/talks/elizabeth_gilbert_it_s_ok_to_feel_overwhelmed_here_s_what_to_do_next (Accessed 2 July 2020).

11. Awaken.org (n.d.) You Were Made for This [Online]. Available at https://www.awakin.org/v2/read/view.php?tid=548 (Accessed on 22 August 2022).

12. The Shift Network (2021) *Andean Shamanic Rituals to Transform Darkness into Light Energy, Interview with Andean Medicine Man Puma Fredy Quispe Singona*, Available at. https://theshiftnetwork.com/Andean-Shamanic-Rituals/recording?utm_campaign=01AndeanShamanism01_20&utm_medium=email&utm_source=maropost&utm_content=01andeanshamanism01_20%20fredy%20%22puma%22%20quispe%20singona%20recording%20+%20fast-action%20expires%202020.11.24&mpweb=708-9181503-742342730 (Accessed 25 January 2022).

13. While this book does not explore the moral precepts of Buddhist thought, a good (and fun) reference on this topic is Hase, C., & Hase, D. (2020) *How Not to Be a Hot Mess: A Survival Guide for Modern Life*, Boulder, Shambhala Publications.

14. In Kornfield, J. (n.d.) *Freedom Amid Challenging Times* [Blog]. Available at https://jackkornfield.com/freedom-amid-challenging-times/ (Accessed on 8 Nov 2021).

Author Biography

Sue Schneider PhD, is a medical anthropologist, integrative health coach and certified mindfulness instructor. She leads community health and wellness initiatives as an Extension Professor and State Health Specialist at Colorado State University and has an integrative health coaching practice in Fort Collins, CO, where she lives with her husband, son and two dogs. To learn more, visit MeetingTheMoment.org.

References

Akomolafe, B. (n.d.) *A Slower Urgency: We Will Dance with Mountains* [Online]. Available at https://www.bayoakomolafe. net/post/a-slower-urgency (Accessed 12 May 2021).

André, C. (2019) 'Proper breathing brings better health', *Scientific American*, 15 January [Online]. Available at https:// www.scientificamerican.com/article/proper-breathing-brings-better-health/ (Accessed 10 March 2021).

Bernhard, T. (2018) *How to be Sick: A Buddhist-Inspired Guide for the Chronically Ill and Their Caregivers*, New York, Simon and Schuster.

Taylor, J. B. (2009) *My Stroke of Insight: A Brain Scientist's Personal Journey*, London, Penguin Books.

Boorstein, S. (1996) *Don't Just do Something, Sit There: A Mindfulness Retreat with Sylvia Boorstein*. San Francisco, HarperSanFrancisco.

Brach, T. (2004) *Radical Acceptance: Embracing Your Life with the Heart of a Buddha*, New York, Bantam Books.

Brach, T. (2012) *True Refuge: Finding Peace and Freedom in Your Own Awakened Heart*, New York, Bantam Books.

Brach, T. (2013) *The backward step*, 13 March [Blog] Available at https://www.tarabrach.com/the-backward-step/ (Accessed 6 April 2021).

Brach, T. (2016) 'Real but not true: Freeing ourselves from harmful beliefs', *TaraBrach.com* [Podcast]. 1 June. Available at https://www.tarabrach.com/real-not-true/ (Accessed 15 June 2021).

Brach, T. (2017) 'Relaxing the over-controller – Part I', *TaraBrach. com* [Podcast]. 26 April. Available at https://www.tarabrach. com/relaxing-over-controller/ (Accessed 12 February 2020).

Brach, T. (2019) 'Two wings of mindfulness', *Lecture for Mindfulness Meditation Training Certification Program*, Opening Retreat, Washington D.C. 15 February.

Brach, T. (2020) Remembering our belonging – Part 1. *TaraBrach.com* [Podcast] 2 December. Available at https://www.tarabrach.com/remembering-belonging-1/ (Accessed 10 January 2021).

Brown, A. (2018). 'How to beat stress, trauma, and adversity with resilience', *Psychology.com*. 23 February [Online]. Available at https://positivepsychology.com/stress-resilience/ (Accessed on 18 June 2021).

Brown, B. (2010) *The gifts of Imperfection: Let go of Who You Think You're Supposed to Be and Embrace Who You Are*, Center City, Hazelden Publishing.

Chödrön, P. (1997) *When Things Fall Apart: Heart Advice for Difficult Times*, Boulder, Shambhala Publications.

Chödrön, P. (2008) *Comfortable with Uncertainty: 108 Teachings on Cultivating Fearlessness and Compassion*, Boulder, Shambhala Publications.

Das, R. (2014) 'Here and now – Ep 16 – Little shmoos', *Be Here Now Network* [Podcast] 15 September. Available at https://beherenownetwork.com/ram-dass-here-and-now-ep-16-little-shmoos/ (Accessed 29 June 2022).

Davidson, R. J., Kabat-Zinn, J., Schumacher, J., Rosenkranz, M., Muller, D., Santorelli, S. F., ... & Sheridan, J. F. (2003). Alterations in brain and immune function produced by mindfulness meditation. *Psychosomatic medicine*, vol 65, no 4, pp. 564–570.

Doty, J. R. (2017) *Into the Magic Shop: A Neurosurgeon's Quest to Discover the Mysteries of the Brain and the Secrets of the Heart*, London, Penguin Books.

Frankl, V. E. (1985) *Man's Search for Meaning*, New York, Simon and Schuster.

Fredrickson, B. L., Cohn, M. A., Coffey, K. A., Pek, J., & Finkel, S. M. (2008) 'Open hearts build lives: positive emotions, induced through loving-kindness meditation, build consequential personal resources', *Journal of personality and social psychology*, vol 95, no. 5, pp. 1045.

Fronsdal, G. (2014) 'Tranquility as a Factor of Awakening', *DharmaSeed.org* [Podcast]. 1 January. Available at https://sr.dharmaseed.org/talks/21898/ (Accessed 3 July 2022).

Goleman, D., & Davidson, R. J. (2017) *Altered Traits: Science Reveals How Meditation Changes Your Mind, Brain, and Body*, London, Penguin Books.

Gunaratana, B. H. (2011) *Mindfulness in Plain English*, Somerville, Wisdom Publications.

Hahn, T. N. (1997) Watering Our Good Seeds [Online]. Available at https://sites.google.com/site/tnhdhamma/Home/test-list/watering-our-good-seeds (Accessed on 27 March 2021).

Hanh, T. N. (2015) *Silence: The Power of Quiet in a World Full of Noise*, New York, Random House.

Hanson, R. (2007) *Seven Facts about the Brain that Incline the Mind to Joy*. [Online]. Available at https://www.rickhanson.net/seven-facts-brain-incline-mind-joy-2/ (Accessed on 13 January 2021).

Hanson, R. (2009) 'Mind changing brain changing mind', *Insight Journal*, vol 32, pp. 9–15.

Hanson, R. (2016) *Hardwiring Happiness: The New Brain Science of Contentment, Calm, and Confidence*, New York, Harmony Books.

Hanson, R., & Hanson, F. (2020) *Resilient: How to Grow an Unshakable Core of Calm, Strength, and Happiness*. New York, Harmony Books.

Hase, C., & Hase, D. (2020) *How Not to Be a Hot Mess: A Survival Guide for Modern Life*, Boulder, Shambhala Publications.

Hougaard, R. (2020) 'The Wandering mind at work: How to go from distraction to deep work', *Forbes*, 14 July [Online]. Available at

https://www.forbes.com/sites/rasmushougaard/2020/07/14/
the-wandering-mind-at-work-how-to-go-from-distraction-
to-deep-work/?sh=5946301b3c65 (Accessed 13 May 2021).

Ikeda, M.P. (2020) 'I Vow Not to Burn Out', *Lion's Roar*, 28
December [Online]. Available at https://www.lionsroar.com/
i-vow-not-to-burn-out/ (Accessed on 15 November 2021).

Jinpa, T. (2016) *A Fearless Heart: How the Courage to be
Compassionate can Transform our Lives*, New York, Avery.

Kabat-Zinn, J., & Hanh, T. N. (1990) *Full Catastrophe Living:
Using the Wisdom of Your Body and Mind to Face Stress, Pain,
and Illness*, New York, Delta.

Kabat-Zinn, J. (2005) *Wherever You Go, There You Are: Mindfulness
Meditation in Everyday Life*, New York, Hachette Books.

Kabat-Zinn, J. (2019) *Mindfulness for All: The Wisdom to Transform
the World*, New York, Hachette Books.

Kornfield, J. (1993) *A Path with Heart: A Guide Through the Perils
and Promises of Spiritual Life*, New York, Bantam Books.

Kornfield, J. (1995) *The Roots of Buddhist Psychology*. Louisville,
Sounds True Audio.

Kornfield, J. (2009) *The Wise Heart: A Guide to the Universal
Teachings of Buddhist Psychology*, New York, Bantam Books.

Kornfiled, J. (2019a) 'Awareness of thoughts', *Transcript of Live
Recording for Mindfulness Meditation Teacher Certification
Program*, Louisville, Sounds True.

Kornfield, Jack. (2019b) 'Mindfulness of emotions', *Transcript of
Live Recording for Mindfulness Meditation Teacher Certification
Program*, Louisville, Sounds True.

Lama, D., Tutu, D., & Abrams, D. C. (2016) *The Book of Joy: Lasting
Happiness in a Changing World*, London, Penguin Books.

Lama, D. (2020) 'Living the Compassionate Life', *Lion's Roar*,
7 July [Online]. Available at https://www.lionsroar.com/
living-the-compassionate-life/ (Accessed on 12 December
2021).

Lion's Roar Staff (2018, March). 'Pema Chödrön & k.d. lang talk Buddhism, creativity, and "gapaciousness," *Lions' Roar*, 23 March [Online] https://www.lionsroar.com/pema-chodron-k-d-lang-talk-buddhism-creativity-and-gapaciousness/ (Accessed on 21 November 2021).

Lyubomirsky, S. (2008) *The How of Happiness: A Scientific Approach to Getting the Life You Want*, London, Penguin Books.

McCue, L. (2009), *Quiet Bunny*, New York, Sterling Publishing.

Mingyur, R. Y., & Tworkov, H. (2019) *In Love with the World: A Monk's Journey Through the Bardos of Living and Dying*, New York, Random House.

Mumford, G. (2017) 'Leading with wisdom', *Transcript of Live Recording for Mindfulness Meditation Teacher Certification Program*, Louisville, Sounds True.

Neff, K. D. (2012) 'The science of self-compassion', *Compassion and wisdom in psychotherapy*, vol 1, pp. 79–92.

Nyima, L. (2020) We're in This Together: Heartbreak and Healing in Difficult Times. 22 September. *Drala Mountain Center* [Blog]. Available at https://blog.shambhalamountain.org/were-in-this-together-heartbreak-and-healing-in-2020-part-i-of-ii/?inf_contact_key=41d74d110b039924bf2ae7c4a066aacdf651f238aa2edbb9c8b7cff03e0b16a0 (Accessed on May 12, 2022).

Ostaseski, F. (2017) *Five Invitations: Discovering What Death Can Teach Us about Living Fully*, New York, Pan Macmillan.

Rosenberg, L. (2004) *Breath by Breath: The Liberating Practice of Insight Meditation*, Boulder, Shambhala Publications.

Salzberg, S. (2002) *Sit* [Online] Available at https://www.sharonsalzberg.com/sit/ (Accessed March 19, 2021).

The Shift Network (2021) *Andean Shamanic Rituals to Transform Darkness into Light Energy, Interview with Andean Medicine Man Puma Fredy Quispe Singona*, Available at. https://theshiftnetwork.com/Andean-Shamanic-Rituals/

recording?utm_campaign=01AndeanShamanism01_2
0&utm_medium=email&utm_source=maropost&utm_
content=01andeanshamanism01_20%20fredy%20
%22puma%22%20quispe%20singona%20recording%20+%20
fast-action%20expires%202020.11.24&mpweb=708-
9181503-742342730 (Accessed 25 January 2022).

Schneider, S. D. (2010) *Mexican Community Health and the Politics of Health Reform*, Albuquerque, University of New Mexico Press.

Shapiro, S. L., & Carlson, L. E. (2009) *The Art and Science of Mindfulness: Integrating Mindfulness into Psychology and the Helping Professions*, Washington, D.C., American Psychological Association.

Shapiro, S. (2020) *Good Morning, I Love You: Mindfulness and Self-compassion Practices to Rewire Your Brain for Calm, Clarity, and Joy*, Louisville, Sounds True.

Siegel, R. D. (2009) *The Mindfulness Solution: Everyday Practices for Everyday Problems*, New York, The Guilford Press.

Siegel, D. (2014) *Name it to Tame it*. YouTube video, added by Dalai Lama Center for Peace and Education [Online]. Available at https://www.youtube.com/watch?v=ZcDLzppD4Jc (Accessed 12 January 2020).

Sood, A. (2013) *The Mayo Clinic Guide to Stress-Free Living*, Boston, Da Capo Lifelong Books.

Spoon, M. (2018) 'Meditation affects brain networks differently in long-term meditators and novices', *University of Wisconsin-Madison News*, 23 July [Online]. Available at https://news.wisc.edu/meditation-affects-brain-networks-differently-in-long-term-meditators-and-novices/ (Accessed on 8 August 2020).

Svoboda, E. (2013) 'Selflessness… or Self-Sabotage?', *Psychology Today* 5 July [Online]. Available at https://www.psychologytoday.com/us/blog/what-makes-hero/201307/selflessness-or-self-sabotage-0 (Accessed 20 April 2020).

Taren, A. A., Creswell, J. D., & Gianaros, P. J. (2013). 'Dispositional mindfulness co-varies with smaller amygdala and caudate volumes in community adults', *PloS one*, vol *8*, no 8, [Online]. DOI: 10.1371/journal.pone.0064574 (Accessed 10 August 2021).

Treleaven, D. A. (2018) *Trauma-Sensitive Mindfulness: Practices for Safe and Transformative Healing*, New York, WW Norton & Company.

Trungpa, C. (2018) 'How everything becomes meditation', *Lion's Roar*, March, p. 53.

Weiss, L. (2018) Cultivating compassion in the workplace [*Presentation for Colorado State University Cultivating Compassion Summit*], 24 April.

Weissbourd, R., Batanova, M., Lovison, V. and Torres, E. (2021) Loneliness in America [Online]. Available at https://static1. squarespace.com/static/5b7c56e255b02c683659fe43/t/60217 76bdd04957c4557c212/1612805995893/Loneliness+in+Ameri ca+2021_02_08_FINAL.pdf (Accessed15 January 2022).

Yeginsu, C (2018). 'U.K. appoints a minister for loneliness', *The New York Times* [Online]. Available at https://www.nytimes. com/2018/01/17/world/europe/uk-britain-loneliness.html. Accessed 12 April 2021.

MANTRA
BOOKS

EASTERN RELIGION & PHILOSOPHY

We publish books on Eastern religions and philosophies. Books
that aim to inform and explore the various traditions that
began in the East and have migrated West.
If you have enjoyed this book, why not tell other readers by
posting a review on your preferred book site.

Recent bestsellers from MANTRA BOOKS are:

The Way Things Are
A Living Approach to Buddhism
Lama Ole Nydahl
An introduction to the teachings of the Buddha, and how to
make use of these teachings in everyday life.
Paperback: 978-1-84694-042-2 ebook: 978-1-78099-845-9

Back to the Truth
5000 Years of Advaita
Dennis Waite
A demystifying guide to Advaita for both those new to, and those
familiar with this ancient, non-dualist philosophy from India.
Paperback: 978-1-90504-761-1 ebook: 978-184694-624-0

Shinto: A celebration of Life
Aidan Rankin
Introducing a gentle but powerful spiritual pathway reconnecting
humanity with Great Nature and affirming all aspects of life.
Paperback: 978-1-84694-438-3 ebook: 978-1-84694-738-4

In the Light of Meditation
Mike George
A comprehensive introduction to the practice of meditation
and the spiritual principles behind it. A 10 lesson meditation
programme with CD and internet support.
Paperback: 978-1-90381-661-5

A Path of Joy
Popping into Freedom
Paramananda Ishaya
A simple and joyful path to spiritual enlightenment.
Paperback: 978-1-78279-323-6 ebook: 978-1-78279-322-9

The Less Dust the More Trust
Participating in The Shamatha Project, Meditation and Science
Adeline van Waning, MD PhD
The inside-story of a woman participating in frontline
meditation research, exploring the interfaces of mind-practice,
science and psychology.
Paperback: 978-1-78099-948-7 ebook: 978-1-78279-657-2

I Know How To Live, I Know How To Die
The Teachings of Dadi Janki: A warm, radical, and life-
affirming view of who we are, where we come from, and what
time is calling us to do
Neville Hodgkinson
Life and death are explored in the context of frontier science
and deep soul awareness.
Paperback: 978-1-78535-013-9 ebook: 978-1-78535-014-6

Living Jainism
An Ethical Science
Aidan Rankin, Kanti V. Mardia
A radical new perspective on science rooted in intuitive
awareness and deductive reasoning.
Paperback: 978-1-78099-912-8 ebook: 978-1-78099-911-1

Ordinary Women, Extraordinary Wisdom
The Feminine Face of Awakening
Rita Marie Robinson
A collection of intimate conversations with female spiritual
teachers who live like ordinary women, but are engaged
with their true natures.
Paperback: 978-1-84694-068-2 ebook: 978-1-78099-908-1

The Way of Nothing
Nothing in the Way
Paramananda Ishaya
A fresh and light-hearted exploration of the amazing reality of
nothingness.
Paperback: 978-1-78279-307-6 ebook: 978-1-78099-840-4

Readers of ebooks can buy or view any of these bestsellers by
clicking on the live link in the title. Most titles are published
in paperback and as an ebook. Paperbacks are available in
traditional bookshops. Both print and ebook formats are
available online.

Find more titles and sign up to our readers' newslett er at
http://www.johnhuntpublishing.com/mind-body-spirit. Follow
us on Facebook at https://www.facebook.com/OBooks and
Twitter at https://twitter.com/obooks.